S*piritus*

ORU JOURNAL OF THEOLOGY

Volume 2   Numbers 1–2   Fall 2017

Spiritus: ORU Journal of Theology
Volume 2   Numbers 1–2   Fall 2017
ISBN: 978-1-9434-8902-2
Copyright © 2017 Oral Roberts University; published by ORU's College of Theology and Ministry and the Holy Spirit Research Center

Each issue is available at no cost for authorized uses at http://DigitalShowcase.ORU.edu/Spiritus/ and may be purchased in print using the "Buy" button at this site.

Spiritus: ORU Journal of Theology is published semi-annually in March and September.

One-year subscriptions may be purchased at the following (2017) rates: US$50 within USA; US$65 to Canada and Mexico; approximately US$80 elsewhere (adjusted, as needed, to cover shipping costs).

Subscriptions begin upon (1) release of the next issue and (2) successful deposit by *Spiritus* of the correct subscription rate and receipt of complete shipping information: subscriber name, full postal address, subscriber email address and telephone number (including international country code prefix). Subscribe at *Spiritus* Subscriptions — ORU COTM, 7777 S. Lewis Ave., Tulsa, OK 74171 USA. (Send subscription correspondence, including address changes, to the same.)

Spiritus: ORU Journal of Theology is indexed through the Digital Commons (https://www.bepress.com/impact-analytics/). *Spiritus* contents may be searched at http://DigitalShowcase.ORU.edu/Spiritus and through any web search engine. (Because another "Spiritus" journal is published by The Johns Hopkins University Press, searches for contents from ORU's *Spiritus* may succeed better by using the full title and subtitle.)

Cover designer: ORU art student Hye Ji Byun, with assistance from Prof. Jiwon Kim and completed by Robert Bubnis of Booksetters.

Interior designer and compositor: Robert Bubnis.

Unless noted otherwise, all photographs are © 1954–2017 by Oral Roberts University. Special thanks to Don Wilson for supplying these to *Spiritus*.

$\mathcal{S}$piritus

ORU JOURNAL OF THEOLOGY

EDITORS
Jeffrey Lamp, Professor, New Testament & Instructor, Environmental Studies
Wonsuk Ma, Distinguished Professor, Global Christianity

REVIEWS & MANAGING EDITOR
Mark E. Roberts, Dean, Learning Resources

EDITORIAL ASSISTANT
Robert Daniel McBain, Doctor of Ministry Candidate

EDITORIAL COMMITTEE
All editors
Cheryl Iverson, Associate Dean, College of Theology & Ministry
Sally Jo Shelton, Theological Librarian & Associate Professor, Learning Resources
Samuel Thorpe, Interim Dean, College of Theology & Ministry

EDITORIAL ADVISORY BOARD
Allan Anderson, University of Birmingham, UK
Corneliu Constantineanu, Aurel Vlaicu University of Arad, Romania
Kwabena Asamoa-Gyuadu, Trinity Theological Seminary, Ghana

UNIVERSITY ADMINISTRATION
William M. Wilson, President
Kathaleen Reid-Martinez, Provost

Spiritus: ORU Journal of Theology . . .

- Publishes studies from all disciplines pertaining to Spirit-empowered Christianity, from established and emerging scholars

- Emphasizes theological and cognate studies and works from and about Christianity in the Majority World

- Reviews pertinent scholarly works and some professional and popular works of merit

- Publishes scholarship to benefit especially Spirit-empowered Christian communities globally.

Find instructions for submitting articles and reviews for consideration at http://DigitalShowcase.ORU.edu/Spiritus/. This site receives all submissions leading to publishing decisions.

Other correspondence (not related to submissions or subscriptions) is welcomed at <Spiritus@ORU.edu> or

> *Spiritus* — ORU COTM,
> 7777 S. Lewis Ave.,
> Tulsa, OK 74171 USA.

CONTENTS

REVIEWS

NEW BEGINNINGS

JEFFREY LAMP

*W*elcome to volume two of *Spiritus: ORU Journal of Theology!* One may ask, "where is volume one?" And one would be right to ask. The first, and until now the only, issue of *Spiritus* appeared in 1985. That single issue constituted volume one. It was a modest offering, consisting largely of in-house contributions from Oral Roberts University (ORU) faculty, as aptly indicated by the full title of that initial effort: *Spiritus: The Journal of the School of Theology.* Precisely why there was only one issue seems lost to history. Nevertheless, after a lengthy hiatus, *Spiritus* is resurrected and signals an exciting new chapter in the story of ORU's College of Theology and Ministry with the Holy Spirit Research Center, this time with a global focus.

Rather than forget the first issue, the editors decided that the journal should stand in continuity with the first effort all those years ago. Thus, with this issue, numbering resumes with volume two. This particular issue will consist of issue numbers one and two, with the semiannual publication schedule, with cover dates March and September, beginning in 2018.

Why another journal? More specifically, why another journal in the Pentecostal-charismatic tradition? In this crowded field, *Spiritus* raises a voice in service to global Spirit-empowered communities, a space that both expresses the distinctive contribution of ORU to these communities and offers itself as a gift to and for them. As distinctive contribution, *Spiritus* is a vehicle that advances the vision of ORU's founder, Oral Roberts, to bring God's healing and the transformative power of the Holy Spirit to "every person's world," so that every person, every community, indeed all of creation, might experience God's restorative power. As gift, *Spiritus* is a forum for theological reflection that actively promotes a global exchange of views, fostering conversation among Spirit-empowered leaders and communities. To these ends, *Spiritus* promotes mutual learning, the exchange of ideas and experiences, and the exploration of new theological domains and approaches from a wide range of multi- and interdisciplinary perspectives, especially from various areas of the globe, including from emerging contexts.

The editorial team envisions *Spiritus* as more than just a place where scholars publish to enhance their curriculum vitae and pave the way for promotion in rank and tenure. There are more than enough such venues. Rather, *Spiritus* is a place where the full gifts and graces of the academy intersect with the missional concerns of Spirit-empowered communities that are at work in the world to further God's kingdom and witness to the full range of God's healing for God's world. So we take the word 'gift' quite seriously. In God's wisdom, God has raised up many voices who seek to bring the efforts and fruits of their scholarly vocations to aid the church as it fulfills its commission to proclaim the gospel in all the world.

On the one hand, this vision entails witnessing to our Spirit-empowered distinctives, in what others before and around us might call "Pentecostal" or "charismatic." We unabashedly and unashamedly own the identifier "Spirit-empowered," not as something that sets us apart, but as something that speaks to the contribution that God in God's providence has provided for the church of Jesus Christ at this time. In this respect, *Spiritus* will help shape the self-consciousness of this people through studies that identify these distinctives and illustrate how they are at work in God's mission in the world.

On the flipside, *Spiritus* will endeavor to show that the Spirit-empowered movements in the world are inextricably connected to the larger church of Jesus Christ throughout space and time. If Spirit-empowered movements settle in ghettos of their own making or set out to separate themselves into sects that have no connection to the church universal, then these movements will have come up short. Early Pentecostal consciousness evidences the notion that this move of God is a gift to the whole church. *Spiritus* will take seriously the idea that the move of the Spirit in the world is not the possession of one group, no matter how explosive its growth. Rather, the journal will offer its studies as gift not only to the Spirit-empowered communities, but also to the whole church of Jesus Christ.

The present issue expresses the editorial philosophy of the journal quite well. Though originating from within the ORU College of

Theology and Ministry and the Holy Spirit Research Center, no more than approximately half of the studies in each issue will come from ORU faculty. Contributions from scholars from around the world as well as from North America will feature prominently in the pages of *Spiritus*. An exciting feature of the journal is the welcome inclusion of at least one study in each issue from an emerging scholar, where those in the midst of their graduate studies lend their voices to the conversation. *Spiritus* invites a wide range of participants from all corners of the Spirit-empowered world to help shape the future of these communities in their missions. This invitation includes reviews of noteworthy books on topics germane to the interests of Spirit-empowered communities.

Of special note is the effort to offer frequent scholarly inquiries into the contributions of Oral Roberts to the church. Among many opportunities for scholarly probing are these: how is it that a Pentecostal preacher with little formal higher education established a Spirit-empowered university; and how is it that a minister known primarily as a tent-crusade healing revivalist had the vision to establish a medical center that sought to merge divine healing and medical science into a holistic vision of God's healing power? Studies about the life and ministry of Oral Roberts will be one aspect of the gift of the journal to Spirit-empowered communities.

Readers will notice on the cover a one-time appearance of the University's fiftieth anniversary seal. Over the course of the past three academic years, the University has marked the fiftieth anniversary of several milestone events: the founding of the University, the admission of the first class of students, and the first commencement ceremony, to name a few. As we bring these celebrations to a close, we mark a new era in the life of the University with the (re)launch of *Spiritus*. *Spiritus* occupies a foundational place in the University's emerging role as a research center among Spirit-empowered communities. It appears first in a series of envisioned institutional efforts, including a Ph.D. program in theology and the growth of an ecology of research and publication. With this issue, we invite all who participate in the scholarly study of the work of the Spirit in the world to come join the conversation.

ORAL ROBERTS
SON OF PENTECOSTALISM, FATHER OF THE CHARISMATIC MOVEMENT

Spiritus 2.1–2 (2017) 5–21
http://digitalshowcase.oru.edu/spiritus/

VINSON SYNAN

Key Words *Oral Roberts, Pentecostalism, charismatic movement*

Abstract

Oral Roberts was one of the most important religious figures of the twentieth century. He was born and raised in the Pentecostal Holiness Church, hence, a "son" of the Pentecostal movement. He first became famous as a Pentecostal preacher who conducted large healing crusades under his huge tent. By the 1960s, he became the best known Pentecostal in the world, founding Oral Roberts University in 1965. In the last part of his life, Roberts became a father of the charismatic movement in the mainline churches through his television ministry. For nineteen years, Roberts was a member of the United Methodist Church and helped lead the charismatic movement in the denomination. In his last years, he and his university strongly identified with the charismatic movement. Thus, the title, "Oral Roberts: Son of Pentecostalism, Father of the Charismatic Movement."

Introduction

*O*ral Roberts was a Pentecostal pastor from Oklahoma who gained fame as a healing evangelist, television personality, and educator. Roberts not only founded Oral Roberts University (ORU) in Tulsa, Oklahoma, but in his lifetime served as a leader in the burgeoning world Pentecostal movement and later as a founding father of the charismatic movement. In the late 1940s, Roberts emerged from the Pentecostal subculture in Oklahoma to become one of the most acclaimed and influential religious figures of the twentieth century. In his long life of ninety-one years, he served as a Pentecostal pastor, a healing tent evangelist, a television pioneer, and the founder of a major university named after himself. He brought Pentecostal healing evangelism to the attention of the American public through his televised healing crusades, his many books and magazines, and, in his later years, through his prime-time programs on national television.[1]

Oral Roberts was born into a movement that was persecuted, denounced, and ridiculed by the public and rejected by the mainline churches. According to David Barrett, the lowly Pentecostals were "more harassed, persecuted, suffering, martyred than perhaps any other Christian tradition in recent history."[2] As a young man, Roberts felt the sting of this rejection but rose above it all during his amazing life and ministry. In school, he and his brother were often called "Holy Rollers," a term he resented. He also had a severe problem with stuttering. As a child, he was derided by his school mates when he could not get out the words he wanted to say. Despite all of this, it was Roberts who, above all others, turned the tide and brought Pentecostals into the accepted mainstream of American society.[3]

Roberts grew up in the Dust Bowl days of the 1930s. Many Okies, as they were called, decided to move to California to escape the poverty they faced in Oklahoma. The most famous migrants from Oklahoma to California were the Tatham family from Sallisaw, Oklahoma. Members of a Pentecostal Holiness Church, the family was immortalized as the Joad family in John Steinbeck's great American novel, *Grapes of Wrath*. In the novel, Grandma spoke in tongues. After arriving in California, the family worked in migrant camps, but later went on to find prosperity in Sacramento.[4]

The Roberts family did not follow the tempting trail to California, but suffered through the dark days of the Great Depression in Oklahoma. His father, Rev. Ellis Roberts, made a scant living through farming and pastoring local Pentecostal Holiness churches in the area of Ada, Oklahoma. Besides, he also held revivals in other Pentecostal

Holiness Churches.[5] Offerings were small, and Pastor Roberts barely eked out a living for his family of seven children. Oral Roberts never forgot the grinding poverty of his childhood.[6]

Oral Roberts: A Son of Pentecostalism

Oral Roberts (born on January 24, 1918; died on December 15, 2009) was born Oral Granville Roberts in Pontotoc County, Oklahoma, the fifth and youngest child of the Reverend Ellis Melvin Roberts and Claudius Priscilla Roberts (nee Irwin). Both parents were ministers of the Pentecostal Holiness Church and members of the East Oklahoma Conference. He was raised in a Pentecostal church typical of the time and place.

The Pentecostal Holiness Church in which Oral Roberts was born and raised was formed out of the Holiness movement that flourished in the last decades of the nineteenth century. The denomination was the result of a merger of two Holiness/Pentecostal churches in 1911 in Falcon, North Carolina. They were the Fire-Baptized Holiness Church and the Pentecostal Holiness Church. The Fire-Baptized Holiness Church was founded by Benjamin Hardin Irwin in 1896 in Iowa. Irwin was a dynamic healing evangelist who taught a "third blessing" (after salvation and sanctification) which he called the "baptism of the Holy Ghost and fire" or simply "the fire." The national church was organized in 1898 in Anderson, South Carolina, with both blacks and women serving as "Ruling Elders." The Pentecostal Holiness Church was pioneered by the Methodist evangelist Abner B. Crumpler, who emphasized the second blessing of "entire sanctification" as taught by John Wesley.[7]

Both churches accepted the Pentecostal baptism in the Holy Spirit as a third blessing and became Pentecostal after being influenced by the Azusa Street revival under the black pastor William J. Seymour. A member of the Pentecostal Holiness Church, Gaston B. Cashwell, brought Pentecost to both churches in 1907, after traveling to the Azusa Street Mission in 1906 and speaking in tongues. All the churches in Oklahoma were originally part of the Fire-Baptized Holiness section of the church.[8]

Oral was raised in abject poverty. On his mother's side, he was descended from the Cherokee Indians and was proud of his Indian heritage in Oklahoma. In high school, Roberts played basketball on his Ada, Oklahoma, high school team and for a short time joined a local Methodist church with his teammates. In 1935 at seventeen years of age, however, he contracted tuberculosis and was bedridden for five months. Some of his family feared that he might never recover. Yet in his darkest hour of despair, Roberts heard a voice telling him about his future: "Son, I am going to heal you and you are to take my healing power to your generation. You are to build me a university and build it on My authority and the Holy Spirit."[9] He was suddenly healed, however, after his parents and his older brother, Elmer, took him to a tent revival. When the evangelist, George W. Moncey, laid hands on him and prayed a healing prayer, he was instantly healed, although it took months for him to totally recover. Roberts soon preached his first sermon and returned to the Pentecostal Holiness Church, where he was ordained in 1936.[10]

In 1938, he married Evelyn Lutman Fahnstock, the daughter of a Pentecostal Holiness minister, a marriage that lasted until her death in 2005. To this marriage was born two sons and two daughters: Ronald, Richard, Rebecca, and Roberta. The Roberts' suffered great tragedy at the early death of Rebecca in an airplane crash and of Ronald, who fell into drug addiction and later committed suicide.[11]

A young man with limitless drive and ambition, from 1941 to 1947, Roberts pastored local Pentecostal Holiness Churches in Enid and Shawnee, Oklahoma, Toccoa, Georgia, and one independent church in Fuqua Springs, North Carolina. In Toccoa, he experienced his first striking miracle of healing when a deacon in his church, Clyde Lawson, was instantly healed after a falling motor had crushed his foot. When Roberts laid hands on his foot and prayed, the man was instantly healed.[12] At this time, he also was becoming one of the most important young ministers in the Pentecostal Holiness Church. With his rising influence, he was elected as a delegate from East Oklahoma to the General Conferences of 1941 and 1945, the highest governing body of the church. He was looked on as a very loyal son of the church with a bright future in the denomination.

Oral Roberts appears in the second row, directly beneath "Church" and the right pillar in this photo of "unofficial visitors at General Conference in Oklahoma City 1945." Courtesy of the IPHC Archives & Research Center.

After returning to Oklahoma in 1942, Roberts attended Oklahoma Baptist University and Phillips University, studying for two years in each school. He never earned a degree, however, since he soon became a traveling evangelist holding revivals in many parts of the nation. In 1947, while pastoring Enid Pentecostal Holiness Church, he felt the call to become a full-time healing evangelist after visiting the meetings of William Branham, whom he admired. His first city-wide crusade was also in 1947, a healing service held in the civic auditorium of his home-town of Enid, attended by 1,200 people. From there, he purchased a tent seating 3,000 persons and began his meteoric rise to prominence in American religious life. The same year he published his first book on healing, *If You Need Healing Do These Things*. He then went to the radio airwaves with a national radio broadcast. He also soon started his own monthly magazine *Healing Waters*.[13]

In one of his earliest tent meetings in Tulsa, Oklahoma, in June 1947, a sniper fired a shot at Roberts that whizzed by just above his head. When the Tulsa press found out about it, stories were written about the incident that appeared in newspapers all over the United States. Overnight, Oral Roberts became a nationally recognized figure. Because of his increasing fame, Roberts was invited by J. A. Culbreth to preach in the famous Falcon camp meeting in 1948. The other invitation was from Joseph A. Synan, who later served as the presiding bishop of the Pentecostal Holiness Church.[14] His healing crusades became so successful that he soon bought another much larger tent seating 12,500 people, which he filled to overflowing. He called it his "tent Cathedral." As the crowds continued to grow, he soon was attracting crowds that rivaled those of Billy Graham, the famous Baptist evangelist. Like Graham, Roberts refused to segregate his crowds on the basis of race. Blacks could sit anywhere in his tent, a striking exception to the Jim Crow segregation practiced in the South at the time.

Most of his followers were fellow Pentecostals who packed his tents and sent huge offerings to support his ministry. Several Pentecostal Holiness members helped Roberts in his early ministry. They were O. E. Sproull, who served as his first Master of Ceremonies for the tent crusades; Collins Steele, who oversaw the moving and setup of the huge tent; Lee Braxton, who helped him organize his radio and television ministries; and Oscar Moore, who helped run the huge Tulsa office. Other prominent Pentecostals from many churches helped in Roberts' tent ministry. Two of them were Bob DeWeese from the Open Bible Church, who assisted him in the healing lines, and Vep Ellis, from the Church of God (Cleveland, Tennessee), who led music and wrote many songs for the Roberts ministry.[15]

In 1951, Roberts helped Demos Shakarian found the Full Gospel Business Men's Fellowship International (FGBMFI), which, in time, attracted millions of men to their monthly meetings, held mostly in hotels. Roberts' ministry skyrocketed in 1955 when he went on national television, attracting a huge audience across the nation. Americans saw Roberts lay hands on thousands of the sick who stood in lines waiting for his healing touch. Many claimed to be healed. Part of Robert's attraction was his dynamic preaching and positive message which emphasized salvation, sanctification, baptism in the Holy Spirit with tongues as initial evidence, the second coming, divine healing, prosperity, and "seed faith" for finances. During his healing ministry, Roberts conducted some 300 crusades in America and around the world. He claimed to have personally laid hands on over two million people. Many historians credit Roberts with playing a major role in the beginning of the charismatic movement in the mainline churches because of his riveting television specials. Many of his critics called Roberts a "faith healer," a term which he hotly denied. He said that Jesus did the healing and not Roberts himself.[16]

Because of his burgeoning ministry, in 1950 Roberts built a modern multistoried headquarters building in Tulsa that became his center of operations. From here, millions of books, tracts, articles, and magazines flowed out to his dedicated followers. He also inaugurated a weekly Sunday morning television program that for thirty years was the number one rated religious program in the nation. In 1956, he began publishing *Abundant Life Magazine,* which, at its height, went to some two million subscribers. In a 1980 Gallup Poll, Roberts' name was known to 84% of the America public. He became the most prominent Pentecostal in the world. In the decade of the 1980s, he published a daily devotional magazine called *Daily Blessing* that went to a quarter of a million subscribers. In addition to this, the 88 books that he wrote sold some fifteen million copies.[17]

Inside the tent of the 1954 Tulsa Crusade. With Oral Roberts (r) on the platform, facing the camera, is Rev. Bob Deweese, Oral's crusade manager.

With this notoriety, Roberts embarked on one of his most ambitious projects, the founding of a liberal arts university. Beginning in 1962, he financed and built one of the most futuristic campuses in the world, naming it Oral Roberts University. In 1960, Roberts had penned a vision for the new university: "Raise up your students to hear my voice, to go where my light is dim, where my voice is heard small, and my healing power is not known, even to the uttermost bounds of the earth. Their work will exceed yours, and in this I am well pleased."[18]

When classes began in 1965, the university was an undergraduate school with one graduate component, the School of Theology.[19] After a few years, the student body grew to over 5,000 in several undergraduate and graduate schools. These included schools of Medicine, Nursing, Dentistry, Law, Business, Education, and Theology. Although teachers and administrators came from diverse church backgrounds, many of the core leaders were from the Pentecostal Holiness Church. Some of these scholars who helped in the early years of ORU were Dr. Raymond O. Corvin, who served as the Chancellor in the beginning and also the first dean of the School of Theology; Dr. Carl Hamilton, who led the university to full accreditation; Dr. Harold Paul, a history professor; and Dr. Paul Chappell, who later led the School of Theology for many years. Other important scholars came from the Assemblies of God, the Church of God, and other Pentecostal denominations.[20]

As time went on and the university began to grow, Roberts became uncomfortable with his identity as a Pentecostal. Of necessity, he was forced to hire professors for his university who came from mainline churches, because there were few Pentecostals with Ph.D. degrees and with administrative experience on the graduate level. Also, records showed that his donor base showed growing income from mainline donors. In fact the largest donor base was from Methodists. Among the mainline administrators and professors Roberts hired were Dr. Howard Ervin, an American Baptist, along with Dr. John D. Messick, Tommy Tyson, and Bob Stamps, Methodists all. Although Messick came to ORU as a Methodist who had once headed East Carolina University, he was raised in the Pentecostal Holiness Church. In time, Roberts' vision began to broaden far beyond his humble Pentecostal origins as he became friends with many non-Pentecostal Christian leaders, including the most famous one of all, Billy Graham.[21]

During these years, the charismatic movement broke out in the mainline denominations, beginning in 1960, under the leadership of Father Dennis Bennett, pastor of St. Luke's Episcopal Church in Van Nuys, California. Soon thousands of ministers and lay people from all the Protestant churches spoke in tongues and created charismatic movements in their churches. In 1967, a similar but unexpected charismatic movement broke out among Roman Catholics at Duquesne University in Pittsburg, Pennsylvania. In explaining the beginnings of this renewal, Father Kilian McDonnell explained that behind every new charismatic stood a classical Pentecostal.[22]

The most important of these was Oral Roberts, whose televised healing crusades came into the living rooms of every American. It was reported that Roman Catholic bishops in New York City, Philadelphia, and Chicago were becoming concerned by the rising tide of Catholics who loved to watch Oral Roberts on TV, and, to their alarm, also sent him large donations, rather than putting them in church offerings. Clearly something was happening in American religious life. This has led some historians to see Roberts as a father of the charismatic movement.[23]

Oral Roberts: A Father of the Charismatic Movement

Roberts reached an early pinnacle of acceptance when he attended Billy Graham's Berlin Congress on World Evangelism in 1966. For years, Roberts and Graham had been close personal friends, but in planning the Berlin Congress, Graham was reluctant at first to invite Roberts, fearing a backlash from his supporters. Graham later wrote about this in his book, *Just as I Am*:

> Whom should we invite as participants to the Congress? We carefully formulated general guidelines, but they did not automatically resolve every issue. For example, the growing charismatic movement, much of it associated with Pentecostal denominations, was somewhat outside of mainstream evangelicalism. We did not bar these denominations from our crusades, but we

did not particularly encourage their participation either; some of their ecstatic manifestations were controversial and disruptive within the broader Christian community. I felt that my longtime friend Oral Roberts, world renowned for his preaching and healing ministry as well as for the university bearing his name in Tulsa, Oklahoma, should be included among the delegates. I was not ready to assign him a place on the program, but I was convinced that his presence would mark the beginning of a new era in evangelical cooperation.[24]

When Roberts accepted Graham's invitation, he went to Berlin with many fears and trepidations. He was a delegate with a seminar on healing as part of the program. At first, he hung out with his church friends, including R. O. Corvin and Bishop Synan. But soon other non-Pentecostals began to befriend him. In the end, Graham invited him to greet a plenary session and lead in prayer. The results were explosive. Roberts' greeting "was an electric moment. When the applause began, pandemonium broke out. They jumped up from every angle and applauded and applauded." But his prayer moved the delegates more and "moved the entire congress."[25] This broke the ice as hundreds of world leaders clamored to meet and thank him for his ministry. It was indeed "the beginning of a new era of cooperation" as Graham had said. Roberts then returned to America with a wider view of the body of Christ and a new sense of mission.[26]

The next year was a momentous one for Oral Roberts, as he planned to dedicate his new and growing university. In the afterglow of the Berlin Congress, Roberts invited Billy Graham as the main speaker at the dedication ceremony. Graham gladly accepted. It was a windy day, as some 18,000 people showed up for the service, which was held outdoors. In honor of his denomination, Roberts invited his bishop of the Pentecostal Holiness Church, J. A. Synan, to read the scriptures. But the star of the day was Billy Graham, who lauded Roberts on his accomplishments and warned the president and faculty that a curse from God might fall on the university if it ever left its biblical moorings.[27]

From that point on, Roberts began a move to remake Oral Roberts University (ORU) from a more narrow Pentecostal school to a university

The Roberts family with Billy Graham at the dedication of Oral Roberts University, April 2, 1967. From the left: Marshall and Rebecca (Roberts) Nash; Richard, Oral and Evelyn, Ronnie, Roberta; Billy Graham.

that would reflect the entire body of Christ. In 1968, Roberts ended his healing crusades. The *New York Times* stated that Roberts' "tent was folded and replaced by a television studio."[28] A hint of things to come was a growing conflict between Oral and his childhood friend R. O. Corvin, dean of the ORU School of Theology since 1963. As the seminary grew, it soon became apparent to Roberts that Corvin's vision was for the seminary to serve as a training center for the Pentecostal churches and more particularly the Pentecostal Holiness Church, to which both Roberts and Corvin belonged. But after the Berlin Congress, Roberts' view had expanded to include all the mainline churches and not just the Pentecostal movement. In 1968, the two men collided several times over the future of the seminary. In the end, Roberts fired Corvin and closed the seminary in 1969. A drastic step indeed.[29]

In the meantime, the Oklahoma Methodist bishop, Angie Smith, a friend of Roberts, invited him to join the Methodist Church. At first,

Roberts did not take him seriously, since there was a wide theological chasm between the more liberal United Methodist Church and the much more conservative Pentecostal denominations. However, eventually Roberts joined the influential Boston Avenue United Methodist Church in Tulsa, which was pastored by Finis Crutchfield. This move was made with the added influence of Tommy Tyson, the Methodist chaplain of the university, and Wayne Robinson, who had already left Roberts' Pentecostal Holiness Church for Methodism. He then shocked the religious world on May 28, 1968, when he was recognized as an elder in the Oklahoma Conference of the Methodist Church. Pentecostals around the world as well as many mainline church leaders were equally mystified by Roberts' unexpected move. He was not re-ordained, however. Until the end of his life, Roberts' ordination remained with the Pentecostal Holiness Church. For a time, Roberts was a favorite preacher at Methodist events in the United States and overseas.[30]

At first, Roberts led a fast-growing charismatic movement among Methodists and was invited to preach in many leading churches

Demos Shakarian, founder of the Full Gospel Business Men's Fellowship International, with Oral Roberts, in the 1970s. The FGBMFI fueled the early charismatic movement, especially among laypersons, although both Shakarian and Roberts were sons of Pentecostalism. Entertainer and charismatic Christian Pat Boone appears to the left behind Shakarian.

and Annual Conferences. In time, the number of Methodist charismatics grew to number some one million in the United States. Oral Roberts, now a professed charismatic, became their hero. To cement his Methodist connection, Roberts re-opened his seminary in 1976, with Jimmy Buskirk as dean of the seminary. Buskirk was a Spirit-filled professor of evangelism at Emory University in Atlanta. Shortly after his coming, the new school was fully accredited, not only by the Association of Theological Schools (ATS) but also by the United Methodist Church as an approved seminary for Methodist workers. In a short time, most of the faculty were Methodists.[31] Moving in another direction, in 1969, after abandoning his healing crusades, Roberts began a series of prime-time television programs that made him a national TV celebrity.[32]

Roberts' most ambitious project was the founding of a hospital in 1981, which he called "the City of Faith." At a cost of $250 million, the hospital consisted of three buildings of 20, 30, and 60 stories that would house a hospital and a research facility that Roberts claimed would "merge prayer and medicine." In raising money for the hospital, Roberts was roundly criticized by the press for claiming to see a "nine hundred foot Jesus" and for saying that Jesus would "take him home" if he did not raise $8,000,000 to finish the project. The money came in, but Roberts' reputation suffered irreparable harm. In spite of heroic fund raising efforts, the City of Faith was forced to close in 1989.[33]

As a result of this and other negative publicity, the leaders of the United Methodist Church became uncomfortable having Oral Roberts as a member of the church. A blow to Roberts came when Buskirk resigned to become pastor of Tulsa's First Methodist Church. Another bitter blow came in 1987 when the United Methodist Church withdrew its accreditation of ORU for the training of Methodist ministers. After this decision, nineteen Methodist faculty members resigned and left the university. A short time later, the Oklahoma Methodists unceremoniously excommunicated Roberts from the United Methodist Church. He was not even notified by the church officials but learned about his ouster in the *Tulsa World* newspaper while eating breakfast at home. After this, Roberts returned to fellowship with his Pentecostal and charismatic friends.[34]

Soon after, Roberts brought Larry Lea, a leading Southern Baptist charismatic pastor, to Tulsa to serve as the new dean of what he now called "the Signs and Wonders Seminary." Later in 1986, Roberts organized a "new fellowship" of charismatic leaders which he called the International Charismatic Bible Ministries (ICBM). Roberts and ORU were henceforth identified with the burgeoning charismatic movement that was sweeping the world. Clearly his Methodist days were over.[35]

As a charismatic school, the university and its School of Theology experienced a boom in enrollment. Seminary Academic Dean Paul Chappell reported in 1987 that "with its clear identity as a Charismatic Bible believing/teaching institution and with a Charismatic faculty, we have grown to be the 34th largest seminary in North America. We are the fastest growing seminary in North America."[36]

In 1993, Roberts turned ORU over to his son Richard, who was not able to attract enough students and money to maintain the quality envisioned by the founder. Despite his best efforts, Richard Roberts was not able to raise funds on the level that his father had done. More and more the university lived on borrowed money, so much so that the debt soared to over $50,000,000. In 2007, Richard was asked to resign and a new president, Dr. Mark Rutland, was installed. Soon afterward, the David Green and Mart Green families of Oklahoma City gave the university over $100 million dollars to save the school. Under the leadership of Mart Green, the campus was renovated, and the board adopted realistic policies that are helping the university become self-supporting.[37]

In Closing . . .

Oral Roberts died on December 15, 2009, at 91 years of age. He was one of the most prominent American religious leaders of his time, second only to Billy Graham. His emphasis on healing and prosperity still inspires millions of Pentecostals and charismatics around the world. In the end, Roberts was the most famous and influential leader ever produced by the Pentecostal Holiness Church. At the same time, he was the one man above all others who brought Pentecostalism to the attention of the world. In his lifetime, Roberts spent his first fifty years as a

Pentecostal, nineteen years as a Methodist charismatic, and twenty-two years as an independent charismatic.

But in a broader sense, Roberts was not only the leading Pentecostal in the world but also one of the most important fathers of the world-wide charismatic movement that swept into all the mainline churches after 1960. By the year 2017, the Pentecostals and charismatics globally numbered some 669,000,000, according to Todd Johnson of Gordon-Conwell Seminary. As one of the foremost historic figures in both movements, Oral Roberts must now be recognized as one of the major Christian leaders of world Christianity in the past century.[38]

Vinson Synan (vsynan@oru.edu) is Scholar in Residence (2017–18) at Oral Roberts University, where he served as Interim Dean of the College of Theology and Ministry in 2016–17. Previously, he was Dean of Divinity School, Regent University, Virginia Beach, Virginia, USA.

Notes

1 The definitive biography of Roberts is David Edwin Harrell, *Oral Roberts: an America Life* (Bloomington, IN: Indiana University Press, 1985). A fine biography by Paul Chappell appeared in the *International Dictionary of Pentecostal Charismatic Movements* (Grand Rapids, MI: Zondervan, 2002) 1024–25. His career in the Pentecostal Holiness Church can be found in Vinson Synan, *The Old Time Power: A History of the Pentecostal Holiness Church* (Franklin Springs, GA: Advocate, 1973, 1998). A critical account of Roberts' life and ministry is Jerry Sholes, *Give Me That Prime-Time Religion: An Insider's Report on the Oral Roberts Evangelistic Association* (Hawthorn Books, 1979).

2 See David Barrett, "The Twentieth Century Pentecostal/Charismatic Renewal in the Holy Spirit with the Goal of World Evangelization," *The International Bulletin of Missionary Research* 12:3 (July 1988) 1.

3 Among all Oral Roberts' books, two were autobiographies. The first was *The Call: An Autobiography* (Garden City. NY: Doubleday, 1972). The more important one was *Expect a Miracle: My Life and Ministry, an Autobiography* (Nashville: Thomas Nelson, 1995). A warm book of memories was written by his daughter, Roberta Roberts Potts, *My Dad, Oral Roberts* (Noble, OK: ICON Publishing, 2011).

4 See John Steinbeck, *Grapes of Wrath* (New York: Viking, 1939), and Dan Morgan, who traced the Tatham family from Sallisaw to Sacramento in his book, *Rising in the West: The True Story of An "Okie" Family from the Great Depression Through the Reagan Years* (New York: Knopf, 1992).

5 Paul G. Chappell, "Granville Oral Roberts," 1024–25.

6 Roberts, *The Call*, 20–26, and Roberts, *Expect a Miracle,* 10–13.

7 See Synan, *The Old Time Power,* 44–92, and Vinson Synan, *The Holiness Pentecostal Tradition* (Grand Rapids, MI: Eerdmans, 1971, 1978) 44–67. Also see Vinson Synan and Dan Woods, *Fire-Baptized: The Many Lives of Benjamin Hardin Irwin* (Wilmore, KY: Emeth, 2017). A major source for these two churches may be found in Joseph E. Campbell, *The Pentecostal Holiness Church: 1898–1948* (Franklin Springs, GA: Publishing House of the Pentecostal Holiness Church, 1950) 192–253.

8 Synan, *The Old Time Power,* 94–113.

9 Roberts, *Expect a Miracle,* 32.

10 Roberts, *Expect a Miracle,* 33–35.

11 Roberts, *Expect a Miracle,* 195–250. Also see Roberta Roberts Potts, *My Dad, Oral Roberts,* 140–162.

12 Roberts, *Expect a Miracle,* 35.

13 Roberts, *Expect a Miracle,* 78–82.

14 Harrell, *Oral Roberts,* 81–82. Roberts always felt that the publicity from this sniping incident was the breakthrough that brought him to the attention of the American public.

15 Harrell, *Oral Roberts,* 80–110.

16 See Vinson Synan, *Under His Banner: History of the Full Gospel Business Men's Fellowship International* (Costa Mesa, CA: Gift Publications, 1992).

17 Chappell, "Granville Oral Roberts," 1025. Harrell, *Oral Roberts,* 116–120.

18 Larry Hart, "The Seminary: A History of Graduate Theological Education at Oral Roberts University" (np, 2016) 3; http://digitalshowcase.oru.edu/theo_history/

19 See the first catalogue titled, *Information for Prospective Students and Other Interested People* (1965) 1–11. The second catalogue titled *Oral Roberts University Bulletin 1966–1967* contained a full list of the Board of Regents, the administration and faculty, and the curriculum for the new university.

20 Harrell, *Oral Roberts,* 211–13.

21 Roberts, *Expect a Miracle,* 315–30.

22 For the beginning of the Episcopal charismatic renewal, see Dennis Bennett, *Nine O'clock in the Morning* (Plainfield. NJ: Logos, 1970). Patti Gallagher Mansfield tells of the start of the Catholic renewal in her *As by a New Pentecost: The Dramatic Beginning of the Catholic Charismatic Renewal* (Steubenville, OH: Franciscan University Press, 1992). For a summary of the renewals in all the churches see Kilian McDonnell, *Charismatic Renewal and the Churches* (New York: Seabury, 1971). Also see Vinson Synan, *Century*

of the Holy Spirit: One Hundred Years of Pentecostal and Charismatic Renewal (Nashville: Thomas Nelson, 2001).

23 Personal conversation by the author with Bishop Synan in Franklin Springs, Georgia, *circa* 1965.

24 Billy Graham, *Just as I Am: An Autobiography of Billy Graham* (New York: Harper, 1999) 536.

25 Harrell, *Oral Roberts,* 204–205.

26 Harrell, *Oral Roberts,* 204–205.

27 Roberts, *The Call,* 203–205.

28 Harrell, *Oral Roberts,* 303.

29 Harrell, *Oral Roberts,* 234–35.

30 Roberts, *Expect a Miracle,* 315–20. The United Methodist "Certificate of Recognition of Orders" for Oral Roberts is in the Oral Roberts University archives in Tulsa, Oklahoma. Roberts was not re-ordained but accepted as an "elder" but not in "full connection." Roberts was a Methodist minister for 19 years. In 1987 he was excommunicated from the United Methodist Church due to rising opposition to his ministry.

31 Roberts, *Expect a Miracle,* 320–23.

32 Harrell, *Oral Roberts,* 235–99.

33 Harrell, *Oral Roberts,* 423–35.

34 Roberts, *Expect a Miracle,* 326–27. The *Tulsa World* stated that Roberts had been "cast out of the Methodist Church by a special committee of leaders." See 328.

35 Roberts, *Expect a Miracle,* 327–30.

36 Hart, "The Seminary" 14–15.

37 See David Green, *Giving It All Away . . . And Getting It All Back* (Zondervan, Grand Rapids, MI: 2017). Also see NBCNews.com, *Businessman Rescues Oral Roberts University,* February 5, 2006.

38 Todd Johnson et al, "Five Hundred Years of Protestant Christianity," *International Bulletin of Mission Research* 41:1 (July 2017) 49.

TRAGEDY OF SPIRIT-EMPOWERED HEROES

A CLOSE LOOK AT SAMSON AND SAUL

WONSUK MA

Spiritus 2.1–2 (2017) 23–38
http://digitalshowcase.oru.edu/spiritus/

Key Words *Spirit of God, Samson, Saul, charismatic leaders, moral failure*

Abstract

This study is motivated by the ongoing dilemma of the ethical failures among well-known leaders of the modern Pentecostal-charismatic movements. Through a close look at Saul and Samson, the two charismatic leaders of the Old Testament who have the most frequent references to the Spirit of God, the study probes the internal and private layers of their experience with the Spirit of God. The intention of the Spirit's presence includes both an internal transformation as well as empowerment for external tasks. The scriptural evidence demonstrates that the internal working of the Spirit is no less important than the empowering outward acts of deliverance. It was these heroes' failure to receive the private and internal transformative work of the Spirit that resulted in their failure.

Introduction

*T*he emergence and growth of Pentecostal and charismatic Christianity are often regarded as contributing significantly to making the twentieth century a "surprise Christian century." Among many positive contributions of the Pentecostal-charismatic movements today, however, bright charismatic "stars" have fallen on moral grounds and have punctuated like deep scars its otherwise glowing face. The problem is, this grave failure is not limited to the "stars" such as megachurch pastors and televangelists: a lax attitude is also observed among less-than-starry leaders in the Pentecostal-charismatic world. Even if the rate of failure is comparable to that of other leaders, it is still a disturbing reality. Why are people who experience the presence of the Holy Spirit no different from those who do not share the same experience? If "empowerment for service" is the main purpose of such spiritual encounters, then would it not be unfair for these leaders to be used as a machine or tool for specific purposes and then thrown away the next moment? If the Holy Spirit is not a force but a person, doesn't this create a serious theological dilemma? This rather disturbing question has led me to notice similar failures among the Spirit-empowered heroes of old.

Samson and Saul are two leaders who have first and second place on the leader board of Spirit-endued charismatic leaders in the Old Testament. Samson records four references to the coming of the Spirit, all positive (Judg 13:25; 14:6, 19; 15:14). On the other hand, Saul has a whopping ten references, but five of them are to "the evil spirit (from God)" (1 Sam 16:15, 16, 23; 18:10; 19:9).[1] Then two refers to the departure of God's Spirit (1 Sam 16:15) and the Spirit's work to immobilise him (19:23). These leave only three references (1 Sam 10:6, 10; 11:6). My immediate inquiry is this: is there any textual evidence to suggest the presence of the Spirit beyond the empowerment of heroes? I decided to limit my search to historical Spirit-empowered heroes, or charismatic leaders, as the future figures such as the ideal king in Isa 11 and the Servant in Isa 42 would represent an ideal type of Spirit-empowered leader(s).

If the Spirit would affect the inner being of the hero, it would have to be in a private setting. Such a case would also be expected at the beginning of the hero's career rather than later. And references then would employ language which would suggest the internal and private effect of the Spirit. In both heroes, such passages are found: Judg 13 and 1 Sam 10. The inclusion of these passages is made possible due to the multiple references by Samson and Saul to the coming of God's Spirit. Understandably, almost no attention will be given to the famous passages which describe their exploits of the enemies. At the same time, this study faces a serious challenge: we are talking about only a few passages, and sometimes the meaning of certain terms is uncertain. This challenge will make it almost impossible to investigate the process and nature of the Spirit's work on the values, spirituality, and morality of a person. At the end, there may be no conclusive outcome.

This study, therefore, will take a close look at the two passages and capture any notion of the Spirit's internal work within the heroes. The study concludes with any implications to contemporary Christian life, especially applicable to Pentecostal-charismatic believers.

Judges 13:24–25

> The woman bore a son, and named him Samson. The boy grew, and the Lord blessed him. The spirit of the Lord began to stir him in Mahaneh-dan, between Zorah and Eshtaol.[2]

The book is structured by what is often called the repetition of a "theological cycle": Israel deserted its God and resorted to other gods, God "gave" Israel to an oppressive enemy hand, Israel sought God in repentance, then God prepared a deliverer (e.g., Judg 2:10–16). This destitute state of the loosely organized tribal alliance is regularly attributed to the lack of a central rule, or king: "In those days there was no king in Israel; all the people did what was right in their own eyes" (Judg 17:6; also 18:1; 19:1; 21:25). In a way, the whole book prepares for the emergence of an Israelite monarchy. Samson is the last judge to be recorded. At the conclusion of the previous judges (in this case, Jephthah followed by three others, Judg 12), strangely the normal theological cycle simply disappears. Conspicuously lacking is the repentance element.[3] Instead, Samson's miraculous birth account is introduced.

The birth of a hero has a certain literary pattern, and Samson's case shares some of its features, including these: the appearance of God's messenger; pregnancy after an extended period of barrenness; child birth through God's intervention; restrictions imposed on the mother, as well as on the child; and above all, God's special plan for the new hero. The chapter also serves to present Samson's call to judgeship. This cascading of extraordinary elements surrounding his birth builds a strong sense of expectation.[4] After all, God gave him a "sound mind and a strong body as he grew to maturity."[5] Now, on what basis commentator Herbert Wolf assumes that Samson is endowed with a "sound mind" is uncertain.

Judges 13:25 records the fulfillment of God's promise of a child and his early years. In this brief statement, God's blessing is upon him. In his growing years, he experiences God's Spirit. In referring to the coming of the Spirit upon Samson, the author of Judges employs a strange word instead of the stereotypical verb, צָלַח, which is quite frequently used in association with the coming of the Spirit. In fact, in all the subsequent occasions when the Spirit of God comes upon Samson, the author employs this common verb. In this first incident of the Spirit upon him, there is a strong sense that the context is in a private setting. No reference is made to anyone else being present when this occurred. A close look at this experience needs to take two components of the text into account: the verb and its effect, and the significance of the locations or the lack thereof.

Verb פָּעַם

Determining the exact meaning of the verb פָּעַם also poses a challenge. Its verbal form occurs only five times in the Old Testament: once in qal or piel form (in the present verse), three times in niphal (Gen 41:8; Ps 77:4; Dan 2:3) and once in hithpael form (Dan 2:1).[6] Nonetheless, its usages are consistent: four of the five times, the term is used with "spirit": once with that of Yahweh, and the others with human spirits. When it is used in relation to the human spirit, the persons are actively influenced or "stirred," in each case by dreams. Pharaoh's spirit was disturbed by dreams (Gen 41:8), and so was Nebuchadnezzar's (Dan 2:1, 3). In these cases, the verb can denote the emotional state of the persons, such as "disturbed" or "agitated."[7] But this can also refer to a more active state, such as "moved, anxious, restless" to learn the meaning of the dream.[8]

Of course, Samson's encounter is with God's Spirit and its effect, and, one may argue, it can be different from other cases. Here are several translations: "to stir" (NIV, NRSV), "to move [him] at times" (KJV), "to drive [him] hard,"[9] "to arouse,"[10] "to direct,"[11] or simply "to accompany" (LXX). Drawing from the passages associated with dreams, a generally disturbing or restless state of mind may be agreed on. Although a dream and God's Spirit may be quite different, both were considered by ancient minds to belong to the spiritual realm. For this reason, David Firth argues that the Spirit's stirring was "in directions he would not have chosen."[12] Wolf contends, along this same line, that the intention of the stirring was for Samson to deliver his people from the Philistine oppression.[13]

However, I would like to argue that this encounter tends to point to a more internal and personal nature of the Spirit's work. First, unlike the subsequent coming of the Spirit upon Samson, there is neither an enemy present nor imminent danger. In fact, this experience may have taken place away from people (as seen below). Secondly, despite its brevity, this is part of the record of his initial "call." In this context, the coming of the Spirit serves to affirm God's call upon the hero, not to empower for a military campaign. In the case of Saul, after his initial encounter with the Spirit in a private setting in this passage, the empowering nature of the Spirit took place subsequently in 1 Sam 11. In this case, the Spirit's presence and its effect served as a sign of God's call to Samson. Thirdly, related to the preceding point, the result of the Spirit's coming in this passage does not indicate anything public, such as a military feat as seen in the subsequent record. Yes, there is no record of the effect whatsoever. Nonetheless, the absence of any publicly displayed action points to the private nature of this experience. Consequently, Wolf's suggestion may have gone beyond the warrant of the text.

Places

In view of extremely insufficient textual evidence, would the place named found in the same verse help us towards the establishment of the internal work of the Spirit? Ancient place names are often hard to identify with accuracy. Mahaneh-dan is a region which includes Zorah and Eshtaol. Zorah is identified as Samson's hometown (13:2). Although the exact location of Eshtaol cannot be established, these two locations were customarily used to identify the extent of the Danite territory. For this reason, these two places appear as a pair, except in 13:2.

In the Samson narratives, the Spirit "stirred" him "between Zorah and Eshtaol," and he was later buried "between Zorah and Eshtaol" (16:31). Although several commentators believe that, unlike Zorah, Eshtaol was an area with no population,[14] the usage in ch. 18 does not support this. In all three references, "men from Zorah and Eshtaol" went out to spy a new land (18:2, cf. 18:8). Later, six hundred men from these two places went out to fight for the land (18:11). Moreover, the passages are clear that these men from the two locations were "all the Danites" (18:2, 11).

It is evident that Danites at this time were in a nomadic state, before moving to the northeast. That is why their oppressors were Philistines, while ch. 18 records their attempt to explore a new territory. Zorah and Eshtaol served as the boundary markers as well as the major towns of the Danite territory. However, there seemed to be an inhabited area between these two major locations, and this is where Samson's references took place. Hence, the first experience of Samson with the Spirit is likely intended to be private due to its location and its circumstance.

Summary

The nature of the internal effect is not apparent beyond any textual evidence. However, one thing is clear: This experience is meant to remind Samson of his life calling and God's lordship. The "stirring" or "agitating" work of the Spirit can easily be perceived as challenging his comfort zone. Combined with God's careful endowment of life's gifts, including his birth itself, he then is truly expected to be a godly hero. Thus, it is not too farfetched to argue for the transformative work of the Spirit at this stage, either in attitude, spiritual and contextual awareness, his life calling or mission, etc.

Butler is right, as are others, that the coming of the Spirit is not an approval of his spiritual condition. But I am not sure if I can completely agree with him that the Spirit does not "fill him with an inner spirituality."[15] Yes, the text does not represent a "transformation" of Samson by the Spirit.[16] However, the current discussion suggests at least the possibility of the inner-working of the Spirit in Samson as he grew. Elsewhere, the work of the Spirit in inner transformation is observed.

For example, in Gideon's case, Firth argues that he was transformed from a "fearful" to a "wise and courageous" leader, although this did not occur immediately after his experience of the Spirit.[17] It was through the radical victory with a small army which can only be attributed to divine work (Judg 7:2).

Then, a lesson drawn by several scholars is worth noting. In spite of God's extraordinary preparation of gifts, Samson failed in character development,[18] and his whole life is marked by tragedy.[19] The victories he achieved through manifestation of his military and physical prowess by the Spirit just amount to "saving his own neck."[20] Furthermore, some threats he had to face were of his own making!

What then was the Spirit doing in the making of this young hero? As with many endowed gifts, I may argue, the coming of the Spirit was to enhance God's giftedness in him, and to challenge him with the encounter of God's reality to contribute to the process of his character development. Then, Bowman is absolutely right: "It . . . appears that divine power is constrained by the exercise of human freedom. . . . Divine success appears contingent upon an appropriate human response."[21]

1 Samuel 10:6–7, 9

[6] Then the spirit of the Lord will possess you, and you will be in a prophetic frenzy along with them and be turned into a different person. [7] Now when these signs meet you, do whatever you see fit to do, for God is with you. . . . [9] As he turned away to leave Samuel, God gave him another heart; and all these signs were fulfilled that day.

This passage records the long process of Saul's accession to kingship. After the book of Judges' portrayal of longing for the appearance of a king in Israel, the books of Samuel picture a rather troubling origin of monarchy. Samuel, who combined the offices of prophet and priest, practically ruled the nation in continuation of the judge tradition. The people's demand for a king was caused by the misbehaviors of Samuel's sons (1 Sam 8:5), and God's consent to the demand marks a new era.

It is natural, though, to expect that the new leader, now called נָגִיד, would follow the pattern of the judges. And the divine appointment accompanied by the coming of God's Spirit is the core of the rise of God's chosen leader. In an extremely private and even secretive circumstance, Saul was now anointed by Samuel into kingship. The passage depicts in great detail a part of the third sign, the experience with the Spirit, which the prophet promised to validate this election.

Before we go any further, there are two small points to clarify. The first is, whether "turning into a different person" (v. 6) and God's "giving him another heart" (v. 9) refer to the same event. Most commentators agree that this is the case.[22] The second is the matter of the order. The prediction is for the "turning into a different person," to take place after all three signs have taken place, but verse 9 places the giving of a new heart immediately after this prediction, that is, before the fulfilment of the signs. This caused some commentators to move this phrase after v. 10.[23] However, many take this as part of the summary statement.

The Nature of Saul's Experience with the Spirit

A number of studies point out a close link between the first monarch and the prophetic movement. In this chapter, we find already that Saul was anointed by the prophet, met by the sons of the prophet, experienced the prophetic Spirit, and even linked with the prophetic guild by a popular saying. But more importantly, the entire "Former Prophets," to which this book belongs, present and evaluate the national history of Israel according to prophetic standards. The prophetic tradition stands "as a refreshing counterpoise to the potential despotism of the monarchy."[24]

The third sign involved Saul's journey to Gibeath-elohim (1 Sam 10:5), where he encountered the "sons of the prophet," coming down from a high (cultic) place, "prophesying," presumably under the influence of the Spirit and accompanied by music. Then the Spirit of God rushed upon him, and he also began to prophesy along with the prophetic guild. The hithpael form of the verb נבא is generally understood as referring to prophetic trance or ecstatic behavior.[25] The presence of music and the absence of any oracular activity also support this interpretation.

Throughout the Old Testament, there are several references to "a new heart" or "a different heart." As "heart" and "spirit" are often used in the Hebrew Bible either interchangeably or parallel with each other, "a new spirit" may be considered in this survey. The psalmist pleads for God to "create . . . a clean heart . . . and put a new and right spirit" within him (Psa 51:10). In three places, Ezekiel declares God's promise for forgiveness and a radical transformation using the same terms. "A new heart I will give you, and a new spirit I will put within you" (Ezek 36:26). In a parallel passage, a different expression is used: "I will remove the heart of stone from their flesh and give them a heart of flesh" (Ezek 11:19). The prophet admonishes Israel, "Cast away from you all the transgressions that you have committed against me, and get yourselves a new heart and a new spirit!" (Ezek 18:31). "A new or different heart" (or "a new spirit") is an exclusive expression for a radical inner transformation to return to God and align to his will. The result of the "new heart" in Ezek 11 is telling: " . . . so that they may follow my statutes and keep my ordinances and obey them" (Ezek 11:20). This radical transformation is all attributed to a divine action, far beyond human behavioral change.

Then in Saul's case, to what does this radical transformation, that is turning to "a different person" or having "a new heart," specifically refer? A number of scholars believe that this refers to the prophetic experience he was to have among the sons of the prophet. For example, in an extremely useful book on the three first kings of Israel, T. Czövek, frequently using Polzin for this passage, argues that there was a sort of prophetic conspiracy to restrict this new kingship under the firm prophetic control.[26] Although a close examination of this point is reserved below, it is less convincing for the following reasons. First, Saul's prophetic experience was temporal, and he was not intended to remain in the company of the prophets. The riddle which was later associated with him ("Is Saul among the prophets?") begs a response, "Of course not." Second, the unusual endorsement recorded in v. 7 (then ". . .do whatever you see fit to do, for God is with you") does not naturally fit the prophetic experience. It may be better suited to a military undertaking. Third, as briefly observed above, the "new heart" throughout the Old Testament clearly points to an inner transformation rather than anything external. And, fourth, the nature of this promise refers to Saul's discretionary action, which is quite different from the invasive and overwhelming (and sometimes demobilizing) nature of the prophetic experience.

Then Saul's experience is "a radical transformation of personality," as Parker rightly argues,[27] that is, an inner transformation. Such a divine blanket endorsement is possible only when a human heart is in a complete alignment with God's will. This also presupposes God's complete approval and his enduring presence. In the spirit of a great degree of ambiguity in the text and also perplexity in Saul's mind, this is a reasonable conclusion we can safely make.

The Role of the Spirit Experience

Then what is this radical transformation for? As introduced above, there has been a strong argument that there was a political motivation to maintain a prophetic control over kingship. Like many others, Czövek acknowledges the ambiguity of the passage both to the readers and to Saul. However, he maintains that the intention of the narrator is increasingly clear: "[he has become] a dupe at the prophet's disposal, created with God's assistance, as 10:9 suggests."[28] Through this process, Saul is no longer "the son of Kish and in his father's service; from now on he will be the son of Samuel."[29] Saul's experience was to demonstrate "how impressive a prophetic power can be."[30] Accordingly, Czövek rephrases v. 7 to mean, "If you listen to me, you will do whatever you like to."[31] Only when Saul was to become both king and prophet, a "double warrant for royal dependence on Samuel" is achieved, thus, achieving the prophet's personal control over the king.[32] This religious experience, according to this interpretation, was a political means to set a paradigm of hegemony for prophetism over kingship.

This perspective puts a strong emphasis on the power dynamic in the formative stage of Israelite kingship. In fact, Samuel viewed the demand for kingship as the people's rejection of theodicy or the political authority of Samuel. However, for the reasons I presented above, it is unlikely that the entire experience, including his experience with God's Spirit, was to keep Saul in the company of the prophets, over which Samuel exercised a decisive control. It is important to be reminded that this is part of the call narrative, and the "rushing" of the Spirit upon Saul is the most critical part of the call process. During the wilderness era, Israel witnessed the link between the "call," the Spirit, and "prophesying." Numbers 11 records Moses' election of seventy elders as his administrative assistants. God authenticated his selection of them by granting the Spirit to them: "[God] took some of the spirit that was on him and put it on the seventy elders; and when the spirit rested upon them, they prophesied. But they did not do so again" (Num 1:25). In this "call" account, the "prophesying" served as a sign of the presence of God's Spirit, which in turn served as a sign of God's election:

> [P]rophesying was perhaps one of the best phenomena which includes objectivity, demonstrability as well as its cultural acceptability among the Israelites. This visible demonstration of the spirit's presence was probably intended to provide an objective sign of God's authentication upon the seventy elders to the people.[33]

In this case, the link between the prophesying and the presence of the Spirit is clear: the former serves as a sign of the latter. In fact, this link is more prevalent within the prophetic tradition. It is hard to suspect, therefore, any political agenda in arranging a prophetic experience, if it is at all possible. I imagine that not everyone who was around the sons of the prophet also prophesied like Saul did.

Parker, on the other hand, hints that Saul experienced the conferral of extraordinary power from God through the Spirit.[34] He may have taken Samuel's command for Saul to journey to "Gibeath-elohim, at the place where the Philistine garrison is" (1 Sam 10:5) as an important clue. However, the passage does not show any military significance of Saul's experience in this place. In fact, the link between the Spirit and military exploit comes in ch. 11. Firth also observes a historical development of the Spirit's role on the charismatic leaders: from the empowerment for deliverance (especially among the judges) to exclusively serving as a sign of God's election to leadership (as in David). According to him, Saul is situated in the middle of this continuum, presumably with a possibility of the Spirit's empowerment for military activities, although less prominent by now.[35] McCarter pays attention to the stereotypical verb used here, "[the Spirit will] rush (צָלַח) upon [you]." The verb is normally used to refer to a military exploit, but here, instead, it refers to prophetic ecstasy.[36] It is therefore not plausible to place the coming of the Spirit as an empowerment for military purposes. The whole narrative of Saul's call including his experience of the Spirit is dominated by prophetic elements, although he was not to be a prophet.

Then the only possible role for the Spirit's coming upon Saul is to authenticate his election as Israel's king through the anointing by Samuel. As observed in Num 11, a human element was affirmed by God through the coming of his Spirit, sometimes with a resultant prophetic experience. And this tended to be temporary and also a behavioral expression rather than an oracular one. In this passage, Samuel's election of Saul now becomes God's election. This sign was essential to the perplexed Saul, as well as to the apprehensive Samuel. The experience must have been striking and radical to Saul, thus serving as a sure sign of God's election (but known only to him and Samuel at this time).

Then, does the Spirit's rushing upon Saul serve only to signify externally the Spirit's presence? The language of the passage adds enough weight to the assumption that a radical inner transformation may also be referred to here. McCarter rightly observes the effect of the Spirit's presence as "a loss of self, or rather, the emergence of a new self."[37] God's blanket endorsement of Saul's subsequent actions (v. 7) is an extremely rare statement throughout the Bible, although some commentators believe it is intended to be an attack on the Philistines.[38] The only comparable ones may mostly refer to the future king or the Servant: e.g., "my servant, whom I uphold, my chosen, in whom my soul delights" (Isa 42:1). In fact, this passage presents stronger evidence than the Judg 13 for the inner transformative work of the Spirit. In Saul's case, as in Samson's, it is also noteworthy that he is naturally a man of exceptional statue and character (1 Sam 10:21-24). With all these elements put together, it is not unreasonable to conclude that the experience with the Spirit, as in Samson, was meant to enhance Saul's personal and character development as a chosen leader of God.

Conclusion

When this study began, it was already suspected that the two passages might not provide sufficient data to draw any reasonable conclusion, and this suspicion proves to be correct. The Samson passage is particularly difficult, for there is only one verse to work with, and the passage abruptly ends the chapter. The Saul passage, on the other hand, presents more information to picture the process of anointing and ensuing signs. However, in both cases, several commonalities are observed:

1. Both passages fall into the same category: Leadership Spirit tradition, which is charismatic in nature;[39]

2. Both have multiple references to the Spirit; thus, they are still better cases to use to look into the inner working of the Spirit in leaders;

3. In both cases, the passages mark the initial experience with God's Spirit in private settings;

4. The subsequent experiences with the Spirit involve military activities;

5. Both had inherited favorable dispositions and upbringings.

6. The coming of the Spirit may serve as a sign of God's election for leadership.

7. This function tends not to include the empowering work of the Spirit for specific tasks.

8. On the other hand, there are textual evidences that the coming of the Spirit in these initial encounters may have a role in enhancing their character development through the realization of divine reality and their calls.

Then what lessons do we learn from this study, and how do we gain a sense to be faithful "people of the Spirit"? These failed charismatic lives suggest several important lessons:

1. As discussed above, the Spirit's coming upon the leaders is not just to turn the recipients into a "fighting machine." On the contrary, we can observe God's careful attention to the "formation" of the heroes before, during, and after the giving of his Spirit;

2. However, the effect of the Spirit's presence is contingent upon the human response or the lack thereof. The character formation

through the Spirit is a joint work between divine and human;

3. Although leaders and prophets are both considered "charismatic" when it comes to the work of the Spirit, it is the leaders who are more susceptible to character and moral failures, which ultimately leads to spiritual (and also national) failure.

4. The seductive nature of political power places the leaders in a more vulnerable position, thus, requiring a higher level of awareness of God and the need for God's intervention to resist this seduction. The experience with his Spirit may be just that.

As we conclude, in spite of our less-than-fruitful efforts to unearth any work of the Spirit in the ethical or character development in the recipients' lives, the strongest argument may come from other cases of the Spirit encounter. The ideal king in Isa 11, the Servant of God in Isa 42, and ultimately the life of Jesus epitomize the highest form of Spirit-empowerment. And another study will form a pair with the current one.

Wonsuk Ma is Distinguished Professor of Global Christianity and PhD program director at Oral Roberts University, Tulsa, OK, USA.

Notes

1 My count is among historical figures, excluding the "Servant," for example, with a good number of references to the Spirit of God in the book of Isaiah.

2 All the scriptural quotes are from New Revised Standard Version.

3 David G. Firth, "The Spirit and Leadership: Testimony, Empowerment and Purpose," in David G. Firth and Paul D. Wegner (eds.), *Presence, Power and Promise: The Role of the Spirit of God in the Old Testament* (Nottingham: Apollos, 2010), 274.

4   Trent C. Butler, *Judges*, Word Biblical Commentary (Nashville, TN: Thomas Nelson, 2009), 331

5   Herbert Wolf, "Judges," in *Deuteronomy, Joshua, Judges, Ruth, 1, 2 Samuel*, Expository Bible Commentary 3 (Grand Rapids, MI: Zondervan, 1992), 464.

6   M. Sæbø, "פָּעַם," *Theological Dictionary of the Old Testament*, vol. 12 (Grand Rapids, MI: Eerdmans, 2003), 43.

7   John Gray, *Joshua, Judges, Ruth*, New Century Bible Commentary (Grand Rapids, MI: Eerdmans, 1986), 327.

8   Sæbø, "פָּעַם," 46.

9   James D. Martin, *The Book of Judges* (Cambridge: Cambridge University Press, 1975), 151.

10   Robert G. Boling, *Judges: Introduction, Translation and Commentary*, Anchor Bible 6A (Garden City, NY: Doubleday, 1975), 226.

11   Firth, "The Spirit and Leadership," 275.

12   David Firth, "The Historical Books," in Trevor J. Burke and Keith Warrington (eds.), *A Biblical Theology of the Holy Spirit* (London: SPCK, 2014), 17.

13   Wolf, "Judges," 465.

14   Trent C. Butler, *Judges*, Word Biblical Commentary (Nashville, TN: Thomas Nelson, 2009), 331.

15   Butler, *Judges*, 330.

16   R. G. Bowman, "Narrative Criticism of Judges," in G. A. Yee (ed.), *Judges and Method: New Approaches in Biblical Studies*, 2nd ed. (Minneapolis: Fortress, 2007), 38–39.

17   Firth, "Historical Books," 16.

18   J. C. Exum and J. W. Wheedbee, "Isaac, Samson, and Saul: Reflections on the Comic and Tragic Visions," in P. R. House (ed.), *Beyond Form Criticism: Essays in Old Testament Literary Criticism* (Winona Lake, IN: Eisenbrauns, 1992), 302.

19   Wolf, "Judges," 465.

20   Wonsuk Ma, "The Empowerment of the Spirit of God in Luke-Acts: An Old Testament Perspective," in Wonsuk Ma and Robert P. Menzies (eds.), *The Spirit and Spirituality: Essays in Honour of Russell P. Spittler* (London: T & T Clark, 2004), 31.

21   Bowman, "Narrative Criticism of Judges," 38–39.

22   For example, P. Kyle McCarter, Jr., *1 Samuel: A New Translation with Introduction, Notes and Commentary*, Anchor Bible 8 (Garden City, NY: Doubleday, 1980), 183.

23   For example, Hans Wilhelm Hertzberg, *I & II Samuel*, trans. J. S. Bowden, Old Testament Library (Philadelphia: Westminster, 1964) , 77.

24   Ronald F. Youngblood, "1, 2 Samuel," *Expositor's Bible Commentary* 3 (Grand Rapids, MI: Zondervan, 1992), 624.

25   The distinction between the two common verbal forms (the other being the niphal form) is not straightforward. See a useful discussion in Robert R. Wilson, *Prophecy and Society in Ancient Israel* (Philadelphia: Fortress, 1980), 137–38.

26 Tamás Czövek, *Three Seasons of Charismatic Leadership: A Literary-Critical and Theological Interpretation of the Narrative of Saul, David and Solomon* (Oxford: Regnum Books, 2006), 57–58.

27 Simon B. Parker, "Possession Trance and Prophecy in Pre-Exilic Israel," *Vetus Testamentum* 28:3 (1978), 272.

28 Czövek, *Three Seasons*, 57.

29 Nico ter Linden, *The Stories of Judges and Kings*, The Story Goes, 3, trans. John Bowden (London: SCM Press, 2000), 95.

30 R. Polzin, *Samuel and Deuteronomist: A Literary Study of the Deuteronomistic History, Part 2: 1 Samuel* (Bloomington and Indianapolis, IN: Indiana University Press, 1989), 105.

31 Czövek, *Three Seasons*, 58.

32 Polzin, *Samuel and Deuteronomist*, 106; also Czövek, *Three Seasons*, 59.

33 Wonsuk Ma, "'If It Is a Sign': An Old Testament Reflection on the Initial Evidence Discussion," *Asian Journal of Pentecostal Studies* 2:2 (1999), 167.

34 Parker, "Possession Trance," 272.

35 Firth, "Historical Books," 19. Also Czövek, *Three Seasons*, 57.

36 McCarter, *1 Samuel*, 183.

37 McCarter, *1 Samuel*, 183.

38 For example, V. Philips Long, *The Reign and Rejection of King Saul: A Case for Literary and Theological Coherence* (Missoula: Scholars, 1989), 207.

39 For this classification, see Wonsuk Ma, *Until the Spirit Comes: The Spirit of God in the Book of Isaiah* (London: T & T Clark, 1999), 29–31.

WISDOM PNEUMATOLOGY AND THE CREATIVE SPIRIT
THE BOOK OF WISDOM IN THE TRINITARIAN ACT OF CREATION

JEFFREY S. LAMP

Spiritus 2.1–2 (2017) 39–56
http://digitalshowcase.oru.edu/spiritus/

Key Words *Wisdom of Solomon, wisdom, spirit, creation, Christology, pneumatology, Trinity*

Abstract

Recent interest in Trinitarian theology has given rise to consideration of the act of creation as a Trinitarian act. Focus on the Father and the Son in the act of creation is abundantly attested in this scholarship. However, consideration of the place of the Spirit in the creative act is somewhat underdeveloped. This article delves more deeply into the Spirit's role in creation by looking at wisdom and spirit language in the deuterocanonical Wisdom of Solomon. In the early chapters of the book, wisdom is characterized as a kindly spirit that brings life and penetrates all things, human and other-than-human, bringing into being all things and sustaining all things. Wisdom of Solomon is often mined as a background source for New Testament depictions of Christ, both in his creative and salvific roles. This article will argue that Wisdom of Solomon, through the convergence of wisdom and spirit language, provides a significant background source for reading the creative work of the Holy Spirit in terms frequently employed in viewing the creative work of Christ. This similarity of depiction in creation further confirms that the act of creation is indeed a Trinitarian act.

Introduction

*E*arly in his career, Jürgen Moltmann noted a lacuna in the burgeoning interest in Trinitarian theology. He lamented that there was a glaring lack of attention paid to the Holy Spirit, a lack evidenced in his own groundbreaking monograph, *Theology of Hope*.[1] He expended extensive effort to address the Spirit in two subsequent volumes, *God in Creation* and *Spirit of Life*.[2] One significant aspect of Moltmann's pneumatology, outlined in these books, is the role of the Spirit in the Trinitarian act of creation.

Genesis 1:2 and Psalm 104:29–30 attest to the role of the Spirit in the original creation and the ongoing sustaining of the cosmos, respectively. However, the Bible more amply attests to the role of God the Father and God the Son in the creation and sustaining of the world. Indeed, it appears that Scripture itself evidences the same lack of emphasis on the Spirit in God's creative work that Moltmann identified in scholarly Trinitarian exploration.

This study will delve more deeply into the Spirit's role in creation by looking at the depiction of wisdom in terms of "spirit language" in the deuterocanonical work Wisdom of Solomon. In the early chapters of the book, wisdom is characterized as a kindly spirit that brings life and penetrates all things, human and other-than-human, bringing into being all things and sustaining all things. Moreover, Wisdom of Solomon is often mined as a background source for New Testament depictions of Christ, both in his creative and salvific roles. This study will argue that Wisdom of Solomon, through its characterization of wisdom as a spirit, might provide a significant background source for reading the creative work of the Holy Spirit in terms frequently employed in viewing the creative work of Christ. This similarity of depiction in creation further confirms that the act of creation is indeed a Trinitarian act.

The study will proceed in two major parts. First, it will examine the depiction of wisdom in Wisdom of Solomon, noting the convergence of wisdom and spirit language in contexts evoking imagery of creation. It will then look to the use of Wisdom of Solomon in Christological discussion, using the motif of wisdom and creation in Wisdom of Solomon to bring Christ and the Spirit together in terms of the creative work of each, suggesting that Wisdom of Solomon functions to depict a wisdom pneumatology that in turn informs a robust Trinitarian account of creation.

Wisdom and Spirit in Wisdom of Solomon

We will examine three sections of Wisdom of Solomon where the figure of wisdom is depicted with spirit language in creational contexts. These sections are: 1:1–8; 6:1–8:6; and 12:1. As is evident, the second of these sections (6:1–8:6) is somewhat extensive and central to the opening section of the book (chs. 1–9), with 1:1–8 serving as a thematic introduction to this convergence of language, and the final brief mention elaborating on themes raised earlier in the book. Following a brief overview of Wisdom of Solomon, we will examine each of these passages in order.

Wisdom of Solomon, often called the Book of Wisdom and abbreviated simply Wisdom, is widely viewed as a work composed originally in Greek in the Second Temple Period, probably somewhere between 100 BCE and 50 CE, by a Hellenistic Jew in Alexandria.[3] Such a reconstruction, obviously, excludes Solomon from actual authorship, and indeed, the work is regarded as pseudonymous in scholarly circles. The book evidences the shift in Jewish sapiential thinking away from the more practical application in daily life of "how the world works" to a more scriptural locus for the search for wisdom, seeing wisdom as active in the history of Israel and in the lives of holy people.[4] Scholars have frequently identified philosophical influences from Middle Platonism and Stoicism, with the book frequently compared on this head with the writings of Philo of Alexandria.[5] Various structures have been proposed for the book, though a natural division seems to be to divide the book into two sections, chs. 1–9 and 10–19,[6] with the first part more closely resembling the Old Testament depiction of wisdom[7] and the second part focusing on the participation of the figure of wisdom in Israel's redemptive history in the Exodus. A further advance of Wisdom of Solomon's depiction of wisdom over the Old Testament is in the highly personified figure of the so-called "Lady Wisdom," leading to the frequent literary convention of capitalizing the word "Wisdom" in identification of the feminine personage. This move vividly dramatizes the participation of wisdom in the lives of individuals and in history, doing so while avoiding casting Wisdom as an entity with independent existence apart from God.[8]

Wisdom and Spirit in Wisdom of Solomon 1:1–8

Wisdom of Solomon begins with a call to the rulers of the earth to devote themselves to the Lord with purity of heart, with the promise that the Lord will be found by those who are faithful (1:2–2). Given that the namesake of the book, Solomon, is the exemplar of Israel's wisdom tradition and is the prototype of the wise king, such a call is not surprising. Verses 3 and 4 describe those whose thoughts are perverse and foolish (v. 3), explaining that wisdom "will not enter a deceitful soul, or dwell in a body enslaved to sin" (v. 4).[9] The first occurrence of spirit language in the book is found in v. 5, where it is said that "a holy and disciplined spirit will flee from deceit," establishing a connection that is found throughout the first section of the book.[10] Wisdom dwells with the righteous. Wisdom is then identified as a "kindly spirit" in v. 6. The adjective translated "kindly" is the Greek φιλάνθρωπον, suggesting that wisdom is naturally drawn to human beings, but will choose to dwell only with those who do not blaspheme God with their words.

With v. 7, the focus shifts to a description of the "spirit of the Lord" (πνεῦμα κυρίου) in terms of that spirit's relationship to the cosmos. First, the spirit of the Lord is said to fill the world. Second, this spirit also "holds all things together." As we will see later, these are qualities predicated of wisdom. This more cosmically-oriented language establishes the grounds for the somewhat more anthropologically-oriented focus of these verses. Because this spirit fills the cosmos and holds all things together, this spirit knows the thoughts that dwell within the hearts of human beings and all the words that fall from their lips, and therefore is in position to mark those deserving divine justice (vv. 6–8).

In this first brief convergence of wisdom and spirit language, some parameters are established for the more extensive discourse that follows. There is a fluidity of language introduced here. Wisdom and spirit are depicted as rightly spoken of together in contexts that speak of the structure of the cosmos and the actions of human beings within that larger cosmos. Of course, the connection of wisdom and spirit is not fully elaborated here; it has only been introduced. But we also see here something that will come to the fore in subsequent discussions, namely, that wisdom and spirit, on the one hand, may come close to being identified with each other, but on the other hand, may also be clearly distinguished from each other. Hence our choice of the word "convergence" to describe the usage of the language, for implicit within the notion of convergence is also a sense of divergence.[11] In this opening passage of the book, wisdom is mentioned by itself in v. 4. Then in v. 6, wisdom and spirit are brought together in a compact construction, φιλάνθρωπον πνεῦμα σοφία. Finally, in vv. 7–8, the "spirit of the Lord" is mentioned by itself. This usage seems to suggest that it is appropriate to speak of each of these concepts separately, but that they also constellate easily and naturally in discussions of how the world is organized and how human beings are to conduct themselves with regard to other human beings and to God.[12]

This opening passage has set some groundwork for the more detailed passage to come in our survey. We turn now to the major discourse in which wisdom and spirit converge with particular respect to the created order, 6:1–8:6.

Wisdom and Spirit in Wisdom of Solomon 6:1–8:6

This large section unfolds as a discourse by the narrator, "Solomon," to those who would rule as kings in the world. In large measure, the section is a call for kings to pursue the path that Solomon followed to gain wisdom in the Old Testament descriptions of his pursuit of and prayer for wisdom (1 Kgs 3:6–9). The passage begins with an exhortation for all kings to heed his words as he will describe wisdom for them, the description of which is intended to increase their desire for wisdom and all her benefits (Wisd Sol 6:1–11). Beginning in 6:12, "Solomon" describes wisdom from the perspective of one who is her lover, describing her benefits in lofty terms (6:12–25). Chapter 7 opens with an "autobiographical" account of his own pursuit of wisdom (7:1–14), emphasizing his single-mindedness in pursuing her above all things, and how in the end in obtaining wisdom he was granted "all good things" (v. 11). In 7:15–22a "Solomon" describes some of the scope of understanding granted him by wisdom, particularly in terms of knowledge of natural phenomena. With 7:22b–30, the focus turns to the role of wisdom in the ordering of the cosmos, and here the convergence of wisdom and spirit language functions thematically in the passage. The passage concludes with a reiteration of the call to pursue wisdom on the basis of wisdom's role in creation (8:1–6). We shall look at each of these sections in some detail.

The first section of the passage, 6:1–11, functions as a call to those who rule, for it is with wisdom that the ability to rule justly and righteously is given by the God. Human rulers are easily given to hubris (v. 2) and in their pride they have not ruled according to the precepts of God (v. 4), and so because of their exalted position in God's economy, they will be judged with greater scrutiny than the lowly (vv. 5–8). For this reason, the wise king entreats others in similar station to hear his words, to become holy, and find the resources to rule as they should (vv. 9–11).

The author's praise to wisdom begins in earnest with v. 12. Wisdom is described immediately as radiant and unfading (λαμπρὰ καὶ ἀμάραντος), and yet is described as imminently accessible to those who would just seek after her, because in truth, she is seeking for those who would welcome her (vv. 12b–16). The pair of adjectives used here speak to wisdom's permanence and immortality.[13] In a climactic progression, the beginning of wisdom leads to desire for instruction, and this is said to be love for wisdom. Love for wisdom leads to keeping her laws in pursuit of immortality. This brings one near to God, leading to the conclusion that the desire for wisdom leads to a kingdom (vv. 17–20). This progression is an example of the literary technique known as sorites, a chaining together of items in a progression that culminates in a surprising climax.[14] Here, the surprise is that the pursuit of wisdom leads to a kingdom. At first glance, this looks like a promise that pursuing wisdom leads to a terrestrial kingdom over which to rule, but in light of v. 21, where it is said that honoring wisdom enables monarchs to rule forever, and recalling v. 4, where it is said that monarchs are in truth servants of God's kingdom, something more seems implied here. Wisdom is more than simply the accumulation of the knowledge and skill for ruling a kingdom on earth; wisdom is salvific. This seems confirmed as well by the ascription of the qualities of wisdom as radiant and unfading, speaking of wisdom's immortality.[15] "Solomon" tells the kings that he will now reveal the mystery of this figure wisdom, where she came from, what she has been doing from the beginning of creation, and what she can benefit them if they will attend to his words (vv. 22–25). Wisdom's eternal qualities are brought into connection with wisdom's role in creation.

What follows immediately is an "autobiographical" sketch of the wise king's pursuit of wisdom (7:1–14), apparently given as a template for all monarchs to follow in their pursuit of wisdom. The opening section speaks of his rather ordinary birth (vv. 1–6), noting that he entered the world like every other human being ever born. He is eminently human, like those he is addressing, and in so arguing, he scuttles any potential objections that he was specially endowed to attain what he has. At this point, he now reveals how it was that he came to know wisdom and attain his stature as the wise king, providing a summary of Solomon's prayer for wisdom in 1 Kings 3:6–9. In Wisdom of Solomon 7:7, he recalls that he prayed to God for understanding, and what was given him was the "spirit of wisdom" ($\pi\nu\epsilon\tilde{\upsilon}\mu\alpha$ $\sigma\sigma\phi\acute{\iota}\alpha\varsigma$). This collocation of wisdom and spirit language shows that this is more than mere mental acquisition; it has penetrated the depth of his being and is now a part of him. He is now endued with wisdom, and his response is that of a lover. He preferred her to everything that a human being might long to possess in life: power, wealth, gems, gold, silver, health, beauty, and light (vv. 8–10). Of course, as the account in 1 Kings 3:10–14 goes on to say, he was given all these things because of his single-hearted desire for wisdom, and he was grateful, though interestingly, he expresses a sort of innocent ignorance of the fact that it was wisdom who gave him these blessings, signaling once more his singular devotion to wisdom alone (Wisd Sol 7:11–12). Again, in devotion to wisdom, he becomes a herald for her blessings, indicating that she will indeed grant these blessings to all irrespective of anyone who will pursue her instruction (vv. 13–14).

"Solomon" now asks God for the ability to share what he has received, noting God's sovereignty even over wisdom (vv. 15–16). Then somewhat surprisingly, as he begins to spell out the substance of what it is that the "spirit of wisdom," given by God, has imparted to him, he goes not into a discussion of what it is that might help his audience rule wisely, but describes wisdom in terms of the orders of created existence. The words bear repeating in full:

> For it is he who gave me unerring knowledge of what exists,
> to know the structure of the world and the activity of the
>   elements;
> the beginning and end and middle of times,
> the alternations of the solstices and the changes of the seasons,
> the cycles of the year and the constellations of the stars,
> the natures of animals and the tempers of wild animals,
> the powers of spirits and the thoughts of human beings,
> the varieties of plants and the virtues of roots;
> I learned both what is secret and what is manifest,
> for wisdom, the fashioner of all things, taught me
>   (vv. 17–22a).

Two observations are noteworthy here. First, the fluidity of language in this section is instructive. In the final line of the quotation, wisdom is said to have taught him, though he prefaced this litany with the affirmation that it was to God to whom he prayed for this instruction to his audience, and that it was via the spirit of wisdom that this was initially imparted. God, wisdom, spirit—the source of knowledge of all things variously and authoritatively ascribed, yet not rigorously defined. Secondly, the connection of God, wisdom, and spirit with the created order is telling. The total scope of creation—cosmic, animal, vegetable, the realms of the human and other-than-human creation—are all in the purview of wisdom's activity and presence.[16] This connection forms the foundation for the praise for wisdom that follows.

Verse 21 actually sets the stage for the description of wisdom beginning in 22. Wisdom is called the "fashioner" of all things. The Greek term τεχνῖτις carries the sense of "craftsman" and is repeated in 8:6 to close out this passage. Intervening in this *inclusio* is a lofty description of wisdom.

The description of wisdom actually begins with a description of the "spirit" (πνεῦμα) that is in her, and that spirit is described in vv. 22 and 23 with a list of twenty-one adjectives that describe the intelligence, power, purity, and trustworthiness of this spirit.[17] The number twenty-one is not accidental; three groups of seven indicate complete perfection.[18]Again, wisdom and spirit are characterized as distinct, yet are closely connected, the one used to describe the other. Wisdom, the fashioner of all things in creation, does so with a spirit depicted with an extensive *pleonasm* that attributes to this spirit deeply personal qualities. And this spirit is said to penetrate "through all spirits" (διὰ πάντων πνευμάτων) who in turn possess like attributes: intelligent, pure, and subtle (v. 23). With v. 24, the focus turns back to wisdom, who is first described as "more mobile than any motion." The Greek πάσης κινήσεως κινητικώτερον parallels one of the adjectives just used to describe the spirit characterizing wisdom, εὐκίνητον, and she also pervades (διήκει) and penetrates (χωρεῖ) all things. This latter verb is the one just used to describe the penetration of the spirit within wisdom through the souls of worthy persons. Wisdom is a "breath"[19] (ἀτμίς) of God's power and a pure "emanation" (ἀπόρροια) of the Almighty's glory (v. 25), a "reflection of eternal light, a spotless mirror of the working of God, and an image of [God's] goodness" (v. 26). Winston notes that the use ἀπόρροια is the earliest use of the term in extant Greek literature to describe wisdom as a direct emanation from God, a bold move for someone writing in the biblical tradition.[20] Together with ἀτμίς, the terms are suggestive of pneumatological overtones, especially in light of the convergence of wisdom and spirit language throughout Wisdom of Solomon. Verses 27–28 then touch on a notion that speaks both to wisdom's transcendence and immanence. On the one hand, wisdom is a self-subsisting entity capable of all things who, while maintaining her own existence with full integrity, renews all things and takes up residence in the souls of the holy to make them God's friends and prophets.

Making things new is the provenance of God's Spirit, as Psalm 104:30 affirms. So the renewal of things constitutes a clear convergence of wisdom and Spirit.[21] Wisdom of Solomon 7:29–30 extols the superiority of wisdom's light to the light of the sun and stars, for even those mighty sources of light are followed, from the perspective of earthly existence, with darkness, but evil does not likewise eclipse wisdom. In this section, the author densely enumerates several characteristics of wisdom that effectively bring wisdom and God together in close relation with each other, drawing on Jewish sources (e.g., Prov 8:22–31; Philo) and Greek philosophy (Stoic and Platonic) to reflect that the work of wisdom is indeed the work of God.[22]

The final segment of this large section, 8:1–6, concludes by reiterating "Solomon's" pursuit of wisdom as that which rulers should emulate. As before, the grounds for the exhortation are framed by appeal to wisdom's activity with respect to the created order. Verse 1 states, "[Wisdom] reaches mightily from one end of the earth to the other, and she orders all things well," with v. 5 identifying wisdom as "the active cause of all things" and v. 6 concluding with wisdom's designation as "fashioner of what exists." The point of the section is simple: if this is wisdom's pedigree, then what could possibly be more worthy to pursue?

Wisdom 6:1–8:6 evidences connections between wisdom and spirit that help us tease out implications for a wisdom pneumatology that speaks to our task of viewing the place of the Third Person of the Trinity in the work of creation. But first, one other brief convergence of wisdom and spirit language requires our attention.

Wisdom and Spirit in Wisdom of Solomon 12:1

"For your immortal spirit is in all things."

To call this brief sentence a convergence of wisdom and spirit language looks to be an overstatement. Spirit language is indeed present, but the term "wisdom" is clearly lacking. Moreover, looking at the context here, the referent for the pronoun "your" is clearly God, and not wisdom, as we saw implicit in the previous major section of our discussion. Specifically, this instance of spirit language occurs relatively early in the major section of the book in which the author provides an interpretation of the Exodus events (chs. 11–19), with particular attention paid to the plague narratives in Exodus.[23] In 11:17–12:2 the focus is on the approach to divine judgment exercised by God toward the Egyptians. Though God did punish the Egyptians severely, it was nevertheless a gradual punishment, occasioned because of God's love of all that God has created, God's mercy, and God's moderation, aimed ultimately at the repentance of the wicked. Here 12:1 provides the rationale for God's moderation in judgment. Despite the gross wickedness of the Egyptians, nevertheless, God strives for repentance of the wicked because God's immortal spirit is in all things.[24]

In a real sense, this brief affirmation brings our discussion of wisdom and spirit language in the context of the created order full circle. To this point, we have seen repeatedly that wisdom and spirit converge conceptually precisely at the point of their respective interactions with the created order. Here, it is overtly stated that it is God's own immortal spirit that pervades all of creation. The verse effectively functions as a conclusion to the preceding argumentation in our discussion. The work of wisdom in creation is the work of God, which is here summed up pneumatologically. The work of wisdom, and the work of the spirit that is found in wisdom, is best viewed as the work of the Spirit of Yahweh, a work firmly anchored, in significant measure, in the presence of God's Spirit in creation. In short, what we have observed in the Wisdom of Solomon is an unfolding wisdom pneumatology.

Christ, Spirit, and Creation in Light of Wisdom of Solomon: Toward a Wisdom Pneumatology

Elsewhere I have argued that Wisdom of Solomon functions as a background source for New Testament Christology, particularly in terms of the place of wisdom in the biblical doctrine of creation, particularly with respect to Colossians 1:15–17 and Hebrews 1:2–3.[25] A passage we have already examined, Wisdom of Solomon 7:22–8:6, in its depiction of wisdom, has several points of connection with these two New Testament passages. We will look at these connections in each passage.

Beginning with Colossians 1:15–17, we find a connection between Christ the "image of the invisible God" in Colossians 1:15 (εἰκὼν τοῦ θεοῦ τοῦ ἀοράτου) and wisdom as an "image of [God's] goodness" (εἰκὼν τῆς ἀγαθότητος αὐτοῦ) in Wisdom of Solomon 7:26. Moreover, Colossians 1:16 states that "all things were created in him" (ἐν αὐτῷ ἐκτίσθη τὰ πάντα), mirroring the notion that wisdom is the "fashioner of all things" (ἡ πάντων τεχνῖτις) in Wisdom of Solomon 7:21 (cf. 8:6) and the "active cause of all things" (τῆς τὰ πάντα ἐργαζομένης) in 8:5. Finally, Colossians 1:17 affirms that "in him all things hold together" (τὰ πάντα ἐν αὐτῷ συνέστηκεν), a thought echoed in language the speaks of wisdom as that which "pervades and penetrates all things" (διήκει καὶ χωρεῖ διὰ πάντων; Wisd Sol 7:24), "renews all things" (τὰ πάντα καινίζει; 7:27), and "reaches mightily from one end of the earth to the other" (διατείνει ἀπὸ πέρατος ἐπὶ πέρας εὐρώστως καὶ διοικεῖ τὰ πάντα χρηστῶς; 8:1). Ideas predicated of wisdom map well onto the portrayal of Christ in Colossians 1:15–17.

Several such connections between the language of Wisdom of Solomon 7:22–8:6 and Hebrews 1:2–3 are evident as well. Most significant are the attributions of creative agency to both wisdom as "fashioner of all things" (Wisd Sol 7:22; 8:6) and the Son as the one "through whom [God] also created the worlds" (δι᾽ οὗ ἐποίησεν τοὺς αἰῶνας) in Hebrews 1:2, and the continuing sustenance of the cosmos to both, where the Son "sustains all things by his powerful word" (φέρων τὰ πάντα τῷ ῥήματι τῆς δυνάμεως αὐτοῦ) in Hebrews 1:3 is parallel to those references cited above from Wisdom of Solomon 7:24, 27; 8:1. Moreover, wisdom, as noted above, is a "reflection" of the light, works, and goodness of God in Wisdom of Solomon 7:26, while the Son is the "reflection" of God's glory in Hebrews 1:2. The word for "reflection," ἀπαύγασμα, provides both a lexical as well as conceptual link between the passages. Finally, the Son is designated as the "exact imprint of [God's] very being" (χαρακτὴρ τῆς ὑποστάσεως αὐτοῦ) in Hebrews 1:3, which advances upon the description of wisdom as the "image of [God's] goodness" in Wisdom of Solomon 7:26. At several points, wisdom and the Son are depicted in similar terms.

It is clear from this brief sketch that by the time New Testament writers began thinking Christologically, Christ's agency in God's creation of the cosmos became a significant component of their thinking. This development is part of a trajectory in conceptualizing God's creative work, from the direct ascriptions of God's activity in several Old Testament passages (e.g., Gen 1:1–2:4a; 2:4b–3:24; Isa 45:18; Ps 104:1–9; Job 38–41), through characterizations in Jewish wisdom literature of wisdom as the agent through which God effects creation (e.g., Prov 3:19; 8:22–31; Wisd Sol 7:22–8:6), to what I have called "creational Christology" in several New Testament passages where Christ or the Son is designated as God's agent in creation (e.g., John 1:3, 10; 1 Cor 8:6; Col 1:16–17; Heb 1:2–3; Rev 3:14).[26] Coupling this trajectory with the broader observation that wisdom theology is largely characterized as creation theology[27] suggests that wisdom, creation, and Christ converge conceptually in Wisdom of Solomon 7:22–8:6.

When this understanding is brought into conversation with what we argued earlier, namely, that we see a convergence in Wisdom of Solomon of wisdom and spirit language in the context of the created order, we see how Wisdom of Solomon 7:22–8:6 functions as a locus that brings to mind a whole complex of concepts: wisdom, creation, S/spirit, Christ. The passage functions as a sort of catalyst that encourages bringing them into conversation with each other. The fluidity of language in Wisdom of Solomon with respect to wisdom and spirit in creation is brought together with later New Testament thinking on Christ's connection with creation in terms used to describe wisdom's role in creation in Wisdom of Solomon. The result is a mix that shows wisdom as a key construct in forming an understanding of how S/spirit and Christ relate with each other and the creation of the cosmos.

We noted earlier Moltmann's insistence that the creative act of God is a Trinitarian act. As we also just noted above, there is a significant trajectory of the portrayal of God's creative act spanning both testaments beginning with creation portrayed simply as the act of God, which, under influence of later Jewish thought on wisdom as God's agent in creation, culminates with the New Testament configuration of creation taking place through the agency of Christ. Here we must understand what Moltmann means by the creative process of God. Creation unfolds in three interrelated phases: original creation, ongoing creation, and new creation.[28] In terms of how this pertains to Christ's role in creation, we need look no further than Colossians 1:16–17, where in a series of prepositional phrases, Christ's role in each of these phases is succinctly explicated. All things (τὰ πάντα) were created (ἐκτίσθη) "through him" (δι᾽ αὐτοῦ), a phrase indicating instrumentality, "in him" (ἐν αὐτῷ), a phrase indicating ongoing sustenance, and "for him" (εἰς αὐτόν), a phrase indicating eschatological redemption.[29] Our survey of connections between Colossians 1:16–17 and Wisdom of Solomon 7:22b–8:6 clearly evidences both wisdom and Christ in the original and ongoing senses of creation as delineated by Moltmann. New, eschatological, creation is not immediately obvious in this section of Wisdom of Solomon, though the climax of the book with its extended treatment of the Exodus and creation's and wisdom's roles in that event may arguably portray a redemptive focus implicit in eschatological new creation, especially in 19:6: *"the whole creation in its nature was fashioned anew."*

How would the role of the Spirit figure into Moltmann's three phases of creation? Here, too, we focus on a trajectory of sorts. We begin with Genesis 1:2, where the phrase אלהים רוח ("wind/spirit/breath of God") is brought into connection with the primordial creation just prior to God's ordering of creation described in terms of the seven days of creation (Gen 1:3–2:3). This רוח "hovers" over the darkness and waters of creation in anticipation of its transformation into order. Here focus is on the Spirit in original creation. Psalm 104:29–30 speaks of the רוח as that which fills creation, giving it life and sustaining all things in existence in ongoing creation. Finally, in terms of new creation, the Spirit is seen in two significant passages where the eschatological new creation is launched when the Spirit is given into the world: the resurrected Jesus breathed the Spirit on his disciples to empower them for their mission in the world (John 20:22) and poured out the Spirit on the Day of Pentecost to demarcate the last days (Acts 2:17–21). The Spirit marks the beginning of new creation and empowers the followers of Jesus to prepare all of creation to realize its eschatological destiny to become the dwelling place of God (cf. Rom 8:18–27). Frank Macchia has reconfigured the Pentecostal doctrine of Spirit baptism to include not just human beings, but the whole of creation as well, such that Spirit baptism is the imparting of the Spirit into the world by the Son who was raised in and by the power of the Spirit, working to "liberate creation from within history toward new possibilities for free, eschatological existence."[30]

So here we have two trajectories, one of Christ and one of the Spirit, speaking in terms of their respective roles in creation. Observing these parallel, overlapping trajectories, Moltmann synthesizes them to formulate his Trinitarian conceptualization of the process of creation. This might be framed epigrammatically in the following: God the Father creates through the Son in the Spirit. Christ mediates creation, while the Spirit represents God's *shekinah* presence in creation, holding all things in life by God's pneumatological presence in the world and moving a suffering creation toward eschatological renewal.[31] It is this Trinitarian emphasis on creation that leads Moltmann to see the Spirit as that through which God is in all things and all things exist in God, what Moltmann labels "immanent transcendence," a construct that enables him to see God as distinct but intimately present within creation.[32]

Conclusion

While the two trajectories described above indeed affirm the roles of both Christ and the Spirit in the process of creation, it seems clear that in both the biblical record and subsequent Christian thought, the role of the Second Person of the Trinity is more fully developed and defended. Still, there is scriptural attestation to the role of the Third Person of the Trinity in the creative work of God, and the necessity of the Spirit's place in creation is affirmed as early as St. Basil the Great, who makes much of the fact that for a word to be spoken, breath is required, thus drawing together the divine Logos, Christ, and the divine breath, the Spirit, in the creative act.[33] What our discussion has sought to do is to find another point of connection that strengthens the notion that creation is a Trinitarian act. The convergence of wisdom and spirit language in the context of creation language in Wisdom of Solomon suggests a pneumatological component in the creation of the cosmos. The observation that Wisdom of Solomon informs the subsequent development of creation as a key component of New Testament Christology, particularly in terms of a common reference to wisdom in creation, suggests that it is appropriate to speak of the Spirit as well in connection with Christ in the creative work of God. We are by no means arguing for a full-blown wisdom pneumatology or Christology, nor of a fully developed pneumatology or Christology of creation, in the pages of Wisdom of Solomon. We are merely suggesting that Wisdom of Solomon offers a bridge of sorts to bring together pneumatological and Christological implications for a Trinitarian understanding of creation.

Jeffrey S. Lamp (jlamp@oru.edu) is Professor of New Testament and Adjunct Instructor of Environmental Science at Oral Roberts University, Tulsa, OK, USA.

Notes

1 Ben Dare, "Foundations of 'Ecological Reformation': A Critical Study of Jürgen Moltmann's Contributions towards a 'New Theological Architecture' for Environment Care" (Ph.D. dissertation, Cardiff University, 2012), 14, identifies an eight-page discussion on the Spirit in the classical work, Jürgen Moltmann, *Theology of Hope: On the Ground and the Implications of a Christian Eschatology*, trans. James W. Leach (London: SCM, 1967) 50–58. Cf. Richard Bauckham, *The Theology of Jürgen Moltmann* (Edinburgh: T&T Clark, 1995) 152; Ryan A. Neal, *Theology as Hope: On the Ground and the Implications of Jürgen Moltmann's Doctrine of Hope* (Eugene: Pickwick, 2008) 73.

2 Jürgen Moltmann, *God in Creation: A New Theology of Creation and the Spirit of God*, trans. Margaret Kohl (Minneapolis: Fortress, 1993); Moltmann, *The Spirit of Life: A Universal Affirmation*, trans. Margaret Kohl (Minneapolis: Fortress, 2001).

3 See Michael Kolarcik, *The Book of Wisdom*, New Interpreter's Bible, 5 (Nashville: Abingdon, 1997) 438–41. David Winston, *The Wisdom of Solomon*, Anchor Bible, 43 (New York: Doubleday, 1979) 20–25, places the date during the reign of Caligula (37–41 CE). Peter Enns, "Wisdom of Solomon and Biblical Interpretation in the Second Temple Period," in *The Way of Wisdom: Essays in Honor of Bruce K. Waltke*, ed. J. I. Packer and Sven K. Soderlund (Grand Rapids: Zondervan, 2000) 213, finds the dating in the time of Caligula persuasive.

4 Enns, "Wisdom of Solomon," 215.

5 For a helpful summary of the evidence, see James M. Reese, Hellenistic Influence on the Book of Wisdom and Its Consequences (Rome: Biblical Institute Press, 1970) 156.

6 See Enns, "Wisdom of Solomon," 223, n4, for references to those with differing division points.

7 Enns, "Wisdom of Solomon," 213–14, notes the exception of focus on the afterlife in Wisdom of Solomon.

8 Jeffrey S. Lamp, *First Corinthians 1–4 in Light of Jewish Wisdom Traditions: Christ, Wisdom, and Spirituality* (Lampeter: Edwin Mellen, 2000), 74–77. The question of whether the depiction of the figure of wisdom has moved beyond personification to hypostatization is hotly contested among scholars, with Karen Jobes and David Winston arguing for the hypostatic depiction of Lady Wisdom as nearly a consort of Yahweh. See Karen Jobes, "Sophia Christology: The Way of Wisdom?" in *The Way of Wisdom*, 233–35; and Winston, *Wisdom of Solomon*, 34–35.

9 Unless otherwise noted, all scriptural translations are from the New Revised Standard Version (NRSV).

10 Winston translates the first line of the verse, "The holy spirit, that divine tutor, will fly away from cunning stratagem." This translation virtually identifies wisdom with the divine spirit. See Winston, *Wisdom of Solomon*, 102.

11 Marie Turner, "The Spirit of Wisdom in All Things: The Mutuality of Earth and Humankind," in *Exploring Ecological Hermeneutics*, ed. Norman Habel and Peter Trudinger (Atlanta: SBL, 2008) 114, sees in these verses that wisdom and spirit are "identified" and "equated."

12 Turner, "The Spirit of Wisdom," 115, sees a similar convergence in the movement of language: wisdom to Spirit to wisdom as a kindly spirit to Spirit of the Lord.

13 Kolarcik, *Book of Wisdom*, 491; Winston, *Wisdom of Solomon*, 153.

14 Kolarcik, *Book of Wisdom*, 491.

15 Kolarcik, *Book of Wisdom*, 491.

16 This elaborates on the description of Solomon's scope of wisdom given in 1 Kgs 4:33.

17 The adjectives are: νοερόν (intelligent), ἅγιον (holy), μονογενές (unique), πολυμερές (manifold), λεπτόν (subtle), εὐκίνητον (mobile), τρανόν (clear), ἀμόλυντον (unpolluted), σαφές (distinct), ἀπήμαντον (invulnerable), φιλάγαθον (loving the good), ὀξύ (keen), ἀκώλυτον (irresistible), εὐεργετικόν (beneficent), φιλάνθρωπον (humane), βέβαιον (steadfast), ἀσφαλές (sure), ἀμέριμνον (free from anxiety), παντοδύναμον (all-powerful), πανεπίσκοπον (all-seeing), and χωροῦν (penetrating).

18 Kolarcik, *Book of Wisdom*, 503

19 The term here is not the lexically possible πνεῦμα, but ἀτμίς, perhaps out of concern to keep the concepts of wisdom and spirit discreet.

20 Winston, *Wisdom of Solomon*, 184–85.

21 Kolarcik, *Book of Wisdom*, 505.

22 Kolarcik, *Book of Wisdom*, 503–505. Cf. Winston, *Wisdom of Solomon*, 84–87.

23 Jeffrey Lamp, *Reading Green: Tactical Considerations for Reading the Bible Ecologically* (New York: Peter Lang, forthcoming) ch. 5.

24 See discussion in Kolarcik, *Book of Wisdom*, 541–42.

25 Jeffrey Lamp, "Wisdom in Colossians 1:15–20: Contribution and Significance," *Journal of the Evangelical Theological Society* 41 (March 1998) 50–51; Lamp, *Greening of Hebrews?*, chs. 2 and 8.

26 William P. Brown, *The Seven Pillars of Creation: The Bible, Science, and the Ecology of Wisdom* (Oxford: Oxford University Press, 2010). Lamp, *Reading Green*, ch. 3.

27 See Roland Murphy, *The Tree of Life*, 3rd ed. (Grand Rapids: Eerdmans, 2002), 118–21; R. J. Clifford, "The Hebrew Scriptures and the Theology of Creation," *Theological Studies* 46 (1985), 507–23; J. D. Levinson, "Observations on the Creation Theology in Wisdom," in *Israelite Wisdom*, ed. J. G. Gammie (Missoula: Scholars Press, 1978) 43–57.

28 Moltmann, *God in Creation*, xiv, 97. For a helpful summary, see David T. Beck, *The Holy Spirit and the Renewal of All Things: Pneumatology in Paul and Jürgen Moltmann* (Eugene: Pickwick, 2007) 111–12.

29 Lamp, *Reading Green*, ch. 3.

30 Frank Macchia, *Baptized in the Spirit: A Global Pentecostal Theology* (Grand Rapids: Zondervan, 2006) 89, 97, 109–10. Others have argued for a similar pneumatological framing of eschatology. See A. J. Swoboda, *Tongues and Trees: Toward a Pentecostal Ecological Theology*, Journal of Pentecostal Theology Series, 40 (Blandford Forum: Deo, 2013) 193–204; Clark Pinnock, *Flame of Love: A Theology of the Holy Spirit* (Downer's Grove: IVP, 1996) 48–51; Leonardo Boff, *Cry of the Earth, Cry of the Poor* (Maryknoll: Orbis, 1997) 271.

31 Moltmann, *God in Creation*, xiv, 97.

32 Moltmann, *God in Creation*, 15–17.

33 Basil, *On the Holy Spirit*, 16:38.

JESUS' MOTHER "TREASURED ALL THESE WORDS . . . IN HER HEART" (LUKE 2:19)

ON USING A SPIRIT HERMENEUTIC TO REFLECT TOGETHER ABOUT MARY[1]

Spiritus 2.1–2 (2017) 57–75
http://digitalshowcase.oru.edu/spiritus/

SALLY JO SHELTON

Key Words *Hermeneutics, Holy Spirit, Mary mother of Jesus, Evangelicalism, Pentecostalism, Catholicism, ecumenism, Bernard Lonergan, Amos Yong*

Abstract

A major issue over which many Evangelicals and Pentecostals differ from Roman Catholics is the status of Mary, Jesus' mother. Evangelicals critique some of the Marian dogmas and practices as excesses that challenge Christ's sole mediation and eclipse the Spirit, while Catholics warn that neglect of Mary potentially leads to failure to acknowledge Christ's full humanity and divinity. This is a proposal to place Spirit hermeneutics into ecumenical service to bridge the gap between the Catholic and Evangelical Marys. The Spirit hermeneutics proposed here is built on Amos Yong's (and other Pentecostal scholars') Word-Spirit-Community epistemology, Catholic philosopher Bernard Lonergan's call to broadened horizons and openness to radical conversion, and Mary's own pneumatic hermeneutic by which she prioritizes listening to the Spirit-inspired words spoken into her life, treasuring those words in her heart, and pondering them and the often bewildering events of her life and that of her Son.

Introduction

*I*n the ecumenical enterprise undertaken by Catholics and Evangelicals since the Second Vatican Council, a major stumbling block continues, sadly, to be the differing degrees of honor granted to Mary, the mother of our Lord, by these communities of faith. Pondering the obstacles that "beset even the most sincere desire" to achieve Christian unity, Yves Congar once predicted that even after a degree of agreement had been achieved regarding justification—historically the quintessential bone of contention between Catholics and Protestants—there would still be "the insuperable wall of ... devotion to the Virgin Mary."[2] This wall may be summarized in terms of Evangelicals' and Catholics' major critiques of each other's stance toward Mary. Evangelicals critique Catholic Marian teachings and practices as excesses that challenge Christ's sole mediation and eclipse the Spirit, while Catholics critique Evangelical neglect of Mary as leading potentially to failure to acknowledge Christ's full humanity and divinity as well as to dishonor the one who said, "from now on all generations will call me blessed" (Luke 1:48). The focus here, though, is not to analyze this wall or gap between these widely divergent understandings of Mary but rather to consider a path by which that gap might be overcome.

I propose that Evangelicals and Catholics, indeed, all who yearn to bridge this Marian gap, consider a Spirit hermeneutic as potentially a fruitful way to find a measure of consensus about Mary. To share such a hermeneutic would be in itself a step toward achieving consensus since it is the hermeneutic that Mary herself used.

The Spirit hermeneutic I propose is similar to that articulated by Pentecostal scholars in recent years, but one that is enhanced by the method proposed by Bernard Lonergan, a Jesuit Thomist who has explicated at considerable length the progressive nature of human understanding. He suggests that accommodating this progressive nature of human cognition in doing constructive theology (or virtually any kind of creative thinking) can eventually culminate in a conversion of love that enables persons to grasp, assess, and, if judged fitting, appropriate another's viewpoint, provided that, in their diligent pursuit of truth, they have first been willing to probe and assess their own perspective and to act accordingly. Essential to the adoption of such a hermeneutic is an ecumenical mentality, a disposition toward wholeheartedly desiring and actively seeking unity of heart and thought while diligently avoiding compromise of truth and faith.[3]

A Pentecostal Epistemology

Foundational to a Spirit hermeneutic is a Pentecostal epistemology. Amos Yong names the sources of knowledge on which such a hermeneutic is built as Spirit-Word-Community. Similarly, Kenneth Archer refers to them as Spirit-Scripture-Community, while Roger Stronstad speaks in terms of Spirit-Scripture-Theology.[4] In Yong's triadic epistemology, Spirit indicates relationality, Word rationality, and Community dynamism. His hermeneutic is a trialectic involving the "continuous interplay of Spirit, Word, and Community." Against prioritizing one source over another, Yong proposes a matrix of overlapping and interconnecting negotiations of meaning to arrive at a trialogical reimagination, or reinterpretation, of the encounter of God with self in the world. For Yong, this reinterpretation is not absolute but rather provisional, i.e., "corrigible, fallibilistic, and open to further inquiry."[5]

The task of constructing an ecumenical understanding of Mary requires a theological epistemology and hermeneutic such as Yong's as well as a method such as Lonergan's. It cannot be limited solely to what is written explicitly in Scripture (Word), for to do so would be to truncate what God says, just as Mary herself could not have heard the angel's words for what they were—a word from God—had she confined her epistemology solely to the Scriptures of Israel (Luke 1:30–33, 35–37). People of the Spirit must listen to the voice of the Spirit whenever, wherever, and however the Spirit speaks. Contra *sola scriptura* or reason alone or historicism alone, a Spirit hermeneutic seeks to interpret the experience of the people of God in every age through the illumination of the same Spirit who inspired the written Word and who continues to inspire its proper interpretation today.

In a Spirit hermeneutic, the three epistemological sources do not act independently but rather interdependently by the Spirit: (1) The Spirit interprets the Scripture, relating it to the tradition of the community of faith and to personal experience. (2) The Spirit interprets personal experience, relating it to the Scripture and to the tradition of the community. And (3) the Spirit interprets the tradition of the community of faith in the light of Scripture and of personal experience. The same Spirit who empowers persons and communities of diverse traditions to seek mutual understanding and theological consensus binds them together in their search for truth through the love of God that they share.

Perhaps the hermeneutic described here seems to prioritize the Spirit over the Word or give undue weight to personal experience or to tradition (which I define here, deliberately redundantly, as the communal memory of the common experience of a community of faith). In fact, I do prioritize the Spirit in the interpretative process because so often the role of the Holy Spirit is downplayed or overlooked. I also understand both experience and tradition in pneumatological terms. The Spirit mediates the believer's experience with God through Word and sacrament and in everyday encounters with nature, our fellow brothers and sisters in Christ, and, indeed, all of God's children. Evangelicals and Pentecostals, though they have not historically called their shared memories or common experiences tradition, now recognize them as such, the point being that Catholics and Orthodox need to acknowledge the tradition of Pentecostals and Evangelicals even as Pentecostals and Evangelicals need to recognize the activity of the Spirit in the older traditions.[6]

Tradition itself is mediated by the Spirit. In fidelity to the principle of *sola scriptura*, Protestants have historically tended to think of tradition as primarily human invention or "innovation," but, more and more, Evangelicals are recognizing that tradition, like Scripture, is pneumatic. Although human persons are instrumental in its expression and transmission, it is the Holy Spirit who continues to speak to the people of God in and through it. In this sense, the Bible itself is the written, inspired tradition of Jewish and Christian experience. James Shelton speaks of tradition as "the Holy Spirit speaking to the church through the church for the last two thousand years."[7] The Orthodox also understand tradition in this pneumatological sense.[8]

Mary's Pneumatic Hermeneutic

The hermeneutic I propose might also be called a "Marian hermeneutic,"[9] in that Mary herself used it: "But Mary treasured up all these things, pondering them in her heart" (Luke 2:19; cf. 2:51).[10] The main verb is "treasured" (*suntēreō*, to preserve together), the participle being "pondered" (*sumballō*, to guard together), the locus of the activity being the heart (indicating a holistic rather than a merely intellectual exercise), and the object being the "sayings" (*rhēmata*), including the Annunciation and subsequent events. Even though Mary does not always understand, she treasures all the events and ponders them in her heart.

Mary's hermeneutic can be understood in terms of Lonergan's cognitive model of a thinking, choosing person, the four levels of consciousness in such a person being experience, understanding, judging, and decision.[11] In Mary's case, as she struggles to understand the unique, revelatory experiences that she undergoes, there is a constant internal dialogue as she mulls them over, arranging and rearranging them in her mind, trying to grasp their significance, then evaluating them in terms of what they demand, how she should act in response to them. Finally, there is the decision stage when, after understanding and judging, the person decides to act, as Mary did when she said, "Let it be to me according to your word" (Luke 1:38). According to Lonergan, it is in such decision-making that a person arrives at a level of self-transcendence and achieves authenticity. I see Mary as modeling this kind of theological thinking and living.

Further, in Mary's view, as in the gospel writers', to grasp the significance of the events that happened to her, they had to be interpreted in light of the Scriptures, which in her time were the Hebrew Scriptures (consider, for example, her dependence on the Psalms in the *Magnificat*). This is the same approach the post-resurrection Christ used when expounding the Scriptures to the two disciples on the road to Emmaus and later to the apostles in the Upper Room (Luke 24:27, 44–46). Therefore, I am proposing that Catholics and Evangelicals look at Mary through the same lens that she, Jesus, and the gospel writers used: the Hebrew Scriptures. This was, in fact, until the Enlightenment, essentially the same way the church itself has historically interpreted the Scriptures. So, in addition to looking at the key narratives in the Christian Scriptures about Mary, in this endeavor to reflect together about Mary, I call upon Catholics and Evangelicals to be sensitive not only to the insights of historical criticism but also to the types in the Hebrew Scriptures that illuminate Mary, since only as we consider her in light of her Son who fulfilled the Law and the Prophets (Matt 5:17–18) are we able to interpret her properly.

This Marian hermeneutic has an epistemology that corresponds closely with that of Amos Yong and other Pentecostal scholars: experiential/pneumatic (Spirit), scriptural/rational (Word), and traditional/communal (Community). If the Church is indeed the community of faith through which we today can hear what the Spirit has been saying for the last two millennia, then its tradition has an epistemological value that cannot be ignored without quenching the Spirit. If we, as an ecumenical family, seek to achieve a fuller mutual understanding of Mary, then we need to listen to what the Spirit has led the Church to understand about Mary rather than clinging solely to the letter of the Scriptures. As demonstrated in my dissertation, there has been a 2,000-year-old tradition of linking Mary to the Spirit.[12]

Mary's hermeneutic is pneumatic as she relies not so much on her own intellect as on the illumination of the Holy Spirit, constantly seeking to learn from the words and deeds of others and from the events as they unfold, all the while remaining humble, admitting when she does not understand, yet always seeking to understand. That is why, on the one hand, she accepts by faith Gabriel's pronouncement as divine revelation, as the very oracles of God, while, on the other, she ponders and probes. In pneumatological terms, she hears the angelic words as the voice of God's Spirit in her heart, interpreting this revelation in light of the Scriptures of Israel and the tradition of the Jewish community of faith to which she belongs.

Intrinsic to this hermeneutic, whether consciously recognized or not, is the profound effect that the tradition in which the faith of the hermeneut has been cultivated has on the interpretation. For most Pentecostals, it is the Evangelical as well as the Pentecostal tradition that typically influences their interpretation. For charismatics, that is, those in the renewal of the various mainline denominations, the tradition varies according to the particular church or community of faith with which they are affiliated. In Mary's case, it is her Jewish understanding of the promised Messiah that forms the basis of her initial interpretation of who her Son is and what his messianic mission will be. Gabriel himself refers to this tradition in recalling God's promise of a king of the house of David whose reign will have no end (Luke 1:32–33; 2 Sam 7:12–13, 16; Ps 89:4; 132:11; Isa 9:6–7; 16:5). However, since it soon becomes evident that her Son's kingship will not be the kind that the Jews had historically envisioned—"my kingdom is not of this world," as Jesus eventually explains (John 18:36)—Mary learns to rely increasingly on the voice of the Spirit as she hears it through the words of her Son and in her own heart as she ponders these things. In time, by observing the direction in which the Spirit is directing her Son's life, Mary slowly begins to glimpse the true nature of Jesus' kingship. It is neither Scripture alone nor the tradition of the Jewish community alone, nor is it her personal experience alone that informs Mary. Her own powers of reasoning and understanding are inadequate for the task, as Luke repeatedly makes clear. Rather it is by illumination of the Spirit upon and through her experience in light of Scripture, tradition, and reason as it aligns with that unpredictable "new thing" (Isa 43:19) that the Spirit is always doing that Mary eventually realizes the true meaning of her Son's mission and her own calling within that mission.

Lonergan's Widening Horizons and Conversion

Mary's experience demonstrates Lonergan's point that an authentic hermeneutic must take into account the gradually unfolding nature of human understanding. Understanding, or reason, is one aspect of the hermeneutical process that, though sometimes not explicitly stated, is integral to the interpretative task.

Progressive Nature of Human Understanding

The progressive nature of human understanding of divine revelation is related to what Henry Newman called the development of doctrine.[13]

It is Lonergan's underlying point in his *Insight.*[14] The first step toward authentic understanding is the "personal appropriation of one's own rational self-consciousness."[15] Once that has been achieved, the search for truth takes place through a series of questions and insights. Whenever an insight is gained, it is then examined for authenticity; once the insight is judged authentic, the hermeneut then has the task of rethinking her position based on the new insight, which then, in turn, brings up still more questions. Lonergan's emphasis is that the quest for truth, for a correct interpretation not only of Scripture but of the events throughout history and in our own life and times, involves continuous adjustments to our thinking as new insights bring the truth into ever clearer, sharper focus. As our horizons widen, so does our understanding.

Dialectical Ecumenism

Lonergan's concept of ever expanding horizons in *Method in Theology* enables us to conceptualize what must happen for those in different traditions to come to a place that they can begin to understand each other's viewpoints regarding Mary or any other point of disagreement. Lonergan speaks of this process as a dialectic, "a generalized apologetic conducted in an ecumenical spirit, aiming ultimately at a comprehensive viewpoint, and proceeding towards that goal by acknowledging differences, seeking their grounds real and apparent, and eliminating superfluous oppositions."[16] Such is the aim of any true ecumenical effort.[17]

Also helpful here is Reformed theologian Heiko Oberman's point that as a part of the task of broadening horizons, theologians need to hold themselves accountable to the "brethren," the community of believers, not limiting "brethren" to the members of their own ecclesial affiliation but rather extending it to "all baptized Christians and baptizing communities, the Christian Churches."[18] Like Lonergan, Oberman is essentially calling for a conversion of the heart toward our separated brothers and sisters,[19] to include rather than exclude one another.

Radical Conversion

For Lonergan, dialectic suggests the possibility not only of a progression of thought, development in doctrine, or widening of horizon, but a total transformation involving a radical "change in course and direction … as if one's eyes were opened and one's former world faded and fell away." From such a transformation, Lonergan says, "emerges something new that fructifies in inter-locking, cumulative sequences of developments on all levels and in all departments of human living." The radical type of conversion that Lonergan envisions is one that "affects all of a man's conscious and intentional operations … [that] directs his gaze, pervades his imagination, releases the symbols that penetrate to the depths of his psyche … enriches his understanding, guides his judgments, reinforces his decisions." This kind of conversion is requisite for ecumenists whose endeavors exceed the capacities of their initial horizons and who eventually realize that merely widening their horizons will be inadequate for the task they have undertaken. Once they come to the realization that their intellectual, moral, and/or spiritual commitments are insufficient, they must decide whether to take the leap into radical conversion.[20]

Such a conversion, Lonergan would insist, is not, first and foremost, a decision of the will. It is a God-given grace. Nevertheless, to appropriate that grace a person must first be open to receive it. Such a conversion involves a change of mind and, more importantly, a change of heart. Lonergan speaks of it as falling in love, specifically, falling in love with God. In the process, not only the theological task but the theologians' entire frame of reference is revolutionized, challenging them to rethink their presuppositions and to reconsider what in the past they have summarily dismissed or simply ignored. For Lonergan, being in love with God produces such a radical conversion that there are no "limits or qualifications or conditions or reservations."[21] Though such a conversion sounds rash, even dangerous, Lonergan emphasizes the importance of first making sound judgments. The implication is that we should not commit ourselves to such a radical change without first undergoing a thorough questioning and assessment process because, obviously, the point is not change for change's sake, but change for truth's sake and, yes, for love's sake. To consent to undergo such a conversion can be described as similar to Mary's unconditional yes to the word she received from the angel.

In an ecumenical quest to understand Mary, as in the Evangelicals' and Catholics' search to find a measure of consensus about Mary, such conversion may well be necessary. As theologians from the different traditions, we need, if not a total conversion, then at least a widening of our horizons, a willingness to set aside our personal preferences and preconceptions long enough to be able to comprehend each other's point of view. Only when we create space in our own minds to think, or at least imagine, the way the other thinks will we be able to achieve consensus or some measure of mutual understanding. Further, I might add, only when we ask God to enlarge our hearts to be receptive to each other as brothers and sisters in Christ will we be in a position to experience the full outpouring of God's love into our hearts by the Holy Spirit (Rom 5:5) that can convert us into persons like Mary who say yes to God unconditionally and who seek his truth unreservedly, regardless of the cost.

Provisional Nature of the Hermeneutical Process

Inevitably, the theological conclusions reached in a hermeneutical process will only be provisional,[22] though not in the sense that truth itself is provisional or variable, but only in the sense that a person's or a community's capacity for understanding or ability to articulate truth always falls short. This is the case since human intellect and language are finite and consequently incapable of fully grasping and expressing infinite truth. However, these limitations need not discourage us but rather spur us to continuously pursue an ever fuller, more accurate grasp of God's truth (Hos 6:3; John 16:13; 1 Cor 2:9–16; 13:12; 2 Cor 5:7).

A Return to the Sources

The Pentecostal hermeneutic is similar in some ways to the kind of hermeneutic that the advocates of *ressourcement* promoted. *Ressourcement* entails a return to the sources—Scripture, tradition, and spirituality— that prioritizes experience and faith including belief in the supernatural over that form of intellectualism that, in contrast, prioritizes empiricism and rigid historicity. While the canon of Scripture held by Catholics differs from that of Evangelicals, who tend to follow the Reformers in this respect, both view the Scriptures as Spirit-inspired. Admittedly, some biblical scholars from both traditions place a higher value on empirical historicity than others, but historicity is only one of the criteria used to establish the interpretation of the biblical writings to the modern church. The Scriptures themselves emphasize that interpretation of Scripture must be based on the illumination that the Holy Spirit bestows.[23]

Raneiro Cantalamessa, preacher for the papal household during and since the time of John Paul II, has also called for a pneumatic hermeneutic, namely, a spiritual reading of the Scriptures that considers both the meaning intended by the human author and that intended by the divine.[24] He recalls the writer of 2 Timothy using the Greek *theopneustos* (God-breathed, 2 Tim 3:16) to refer to the theandric nature of Scripture, not only pointing to a dual authorship (human and divine) but also calling for a dual reading (literal and spiritual) of the text. Such a reading is one that looks not only back on the Hebrew Scriptures but forward to what the Holy Spirit has continued to do and say in the church up to the present. Referring to de Lubac's words written prior to Vatican II that it would take a "spiritual movement" to allow the church today to retrieve the spiritual exegesis practiced by the early Christian theologians,[25] Cantalamessa says:

> Looking back at these words after some decades and with Vatican II between us, it seems to me that they are prophetic. That "spiritual movement" and that "élan" have begun to resurface, but not because men have programmed or foreseen them, but because from the four winds the Spirit has begun unexpectedly to blow again upon the dried up bones. Contemporaneously with the reappearance of the gifts, we also witness the reappearance of the spiritual reading of the Bible and this too is a fruit—one of the more exquisite—of the Spirit.

Cantalamessa describes the kind of scriptural reading I propose here, one that recognizes Christ in the Scriptures and that listens to what the Spirit has continued to say about him throughout the centuries, including recognizing in retrospect the mothers of the faith such as Sarah as antetypes of spiritual motherhood that anticipate the role of the mother of the Messiah. This is the kind of interpretation that Cantalamessa refers to in describing what he hears while participating in Bible study groups:

> I am stupefied in hearing, at times, reflections on God's word that are analogous to those offered by Origen, Augustine or Gregory the Great in their time, even if it is in a more simple language. The words about the temple, the "tent of David," about Jerusalem destroyed and rebuilt after the exile, are applied, in all simplicity, to the Church, to Mary, to one's own community and personal life.[26]

In this spiritual exegesis emerging from the scriptural reflections of the lay faithful can be discerned a move of the Spirit that is freeing them from the limits of scientific and historical criticism to allow them to receive a living word from the Spirit of God to the Church and the world of today.

"All These with One Accord" (Acts 1:14): An Ecumenical Mary

The Spirit hermeneutic proposed here is essentially an ecumenical one. When I became Catholic over twenty years ago, I did not, indeed, could not, leave my Pentecostalism behind because it was such an integral part of who I was and still am. My longing for Christian unity continues to grow only stronger after experiencing firsthand the soul-piercing pain that the divisions in the church bring, especially for those who dare to cross the bridges that ecumenism purports to build as well as for their families and friends.

This hermeneutic is built on a love for the Scriptures, both the Hebrew and the Christian—for Christians, the God of Abraham, Isaac, and Jacob is indeed the God and Father of our Lord Jesus Christ—and for the Christian tradition through which the voice of the Spirit has been heard over the centuries. It is built also on the marriage of spirituality with theology, so that it can be fruitful; for apart from the love of God, theologizing, like tongues, is merely "a noisy gong or a clanging cymbal" (1 Cor 13:1). Finally, this hermeneutic is built on the personal disposition of persons, whether theologians or biblical scholars or practitioners, clergy or lay, to remain open to conversion, like Mary, to make every effort to respond to the voice of the Spirit as spoken to this present generation as well as to past generations, regardless of the cost. Clearly, Lonergan's call to a conversion of love is essential not only for finding consensus about Mary but also for the entire ecumenical effort.

The attempt to find a Mary we can all love and honor together is obviously no easy task. Lonergan underscores the difficulty of overcoming cultural inheritances in ecumenical undertakings by explaining that sooner or later dialogues reach a stopping point since participants' traditions ultimately present seemingly impassable obstacles. Though dialogue partners can achieve a degree of respect for the other's position, they typically still consider it wrong. Understanding this helps me to be more realistic about what an ecumenical hermeneutic in and of itself can achieve. Nevertheless, Lonergan's frequent reminders of the key role of conversion in the theological process are, in themselves, an admission that, provided people are receptive and willing, the Spirit of God can and does change hearts and minds despite what, humanly speaking, are insurmountable cultural impasses.

Treasures Old and New

The hermeneutic proposed here is one that grounds any attempt at theological construction not on the *Zeitgeist* but primarily on the treasures of the church. Theologians should be like the wise scribe whom Jesus described as drawing from his storehouse treasures both old and new (Matt 13:52). A term for this approach was coined by theologians of the so-called school of *la nouvelle théologie*, *ressourcement*, mentioned earlier. It is "a return to the sources," namely, to the Scriptures and to patristics, that is, the theologians who have spoken over the centuries. My own interest in *ressourcement* has nothing to do with a reaction against neo-Scholasticism as apparently was the case of the first proponents of *ressourcement*. Rather it is based on the recognition of the foundational place that Scripture has in Christian theology as well as the appreciation I have acquired for the church fathers and mothers and other sources of the great tradition. The Scriptures must be interpreted not only through the lens of the church today but through that of the church of the last 2,000 years.[27] To disregard what the church has said for the last 2,000 years is, in effect, to disregard the voice of the Holy Spirit throughout that time or else to suggest that the Holy Spirit stopped speaking during that time. I make this point not to deny the full revelation of God in Jesus Christ,[28] but rather to recall what Christ told his disciples before his departure: that though he still had many things to tell them, they could not bear them yet, but when the Spirit of truth came, he would guide them into all truth (John 16:12–13).

Synthesis of Faith and Reason

The marriage of theology and spirituality that is part of a Spirit hermeneutic is essentially doing theology on our knees, or, as von Balthasar calls it, "kneeling theology," or, as Wainwright describes it, "doing the theological task in a liturgical perspective."[29] Anselm refers to it as "faith seeking understanding." It is the recognition that faith and reason are both integral to theology. Lonergan speaks of it as a synthesis: "If one is not to affirm reason at the expense of faith or faith at the expense of reason, one is called upon both to produce a synthesis that unites two orders of truth and to give evidence of a successful symbiosis of two principles of knowledge."[30] In other words, reason alone is inadequate for the theological task; nevertheless, although faith always has precedence, reason is still essential since it is a God-given aspect of our humanity, an integral part of the *imago dei* that makes us unique in creation.

Conversion of Heart and Mind

Saying yes to the call to conversion of mind and heart involves continuous repentance: the recognition of the constant need to repent in terms of our attitude toward each other, particularly our lack of humility and charity that makes us think that we are better than the other, or at least that we know better than the other (Phil 2:1–4).

The Marian problematic, as Congar so accurately assessed it, cannot be resolved simply by attaining a degree of theological consensus regarding her. It requires conversion, a change of mind *and* heart. Intellectually, it involves rejection of excess on the one hand and neglect on the other. Spiritually, it involves *rapprochement*, cultivating friendships, praying together, and listening to each other's viewpoints in "a spirit free of rancor, distrust, prejudice, and narrow-mindedness."[31] Lonergan speaks of love preceding knowledge and of the role it plays in ecumenism.[32] It is God's love for us and ours for God that inspires our love for each other and motivates us to seek common ground on which to build intellectual consensus with those from whom we have been separated for centuries. Ratzinger called for a change of heart toward those with whom we differ. For him, Christian unity requires more than reason:

> It presupposes spiritual experience, penance [concrete acts of repentance], and conversion. ... It begins quite concretely by overcoming mutual mistrust, the sociologically rooted defensive attitude against what is strange, belonging to another, and that we constantly take the Lord, whom after all we are seeking, more seriously than we take ourselves. He is our unity, what we have in common—no, who is the one who is common to and in all denominations.[33]

Ratzinger's reference to Jesus as the focal point of Christian unity leads to the question as to whether Mary too can become a point of unity. I would say, yes, Mary can, *if* Catholics and Evangelicals will listen to each other's heart—in the spirit of her own pondering in her heart—about what they believe about her and why and *if* they will listen for the voice of the Holy Spirit speaking through the church over the centuries and through their beloved, though separated, brothers and sisters in Christ today. Adopting the same pneumatic hermeneutic Mary herself used will provide an authentic basis upon which Evangelicals and Catholics can together honor this blessed woman as mother of the incarnate Son of God and, in some nuanced sense at least, as our shared mother in the faith and exemplar of life in the Spirit. Further, using Mary's hermeneutic will provide a means by which we can reflect together about what the Holy Spirit has revealed in the Scriptures and in our respective traditions, so that, in time, we can bridge that gap in our thinking about her that has separated us too long.

Sally Jo Shelton (sshelton@oru.edu) is a Charismatic Catholic with Pentecostal roots and Theological Librarian and Associate Professor of Learning Resources, Oral Roberts University, Tulsa, OK, USA.

Notes

1 Adapted from my "Overshadowed by the Spirit: Mary, Mother of Our Lord, Prototype of Spirit-Baptized Humanity" (PhD diss.: Regent University, 2016).

2 Yves Congar, "Conquering Our Enmities," in *Steps to Christian Unity*, ed. John A. O'Brien (Garden City, N.Y.: Doubleday, 1964) 100.

3 Based on the premise that those accept "the decision in faith of the ancient Church" that the book of documents which we call the Bible is the Word of God and will read it "in intrinsic conjunction with the baptismal creed of the ancient Church" and recognize once again "the real claim it involves, it should not be too long before all sides can distinguish between essential and non-essential and so find the way to a diversified, pluriform unity."

4 Amos Yong, *Spirit-Word-Community: Theological Hermeneutics in Trinitarian Perspective* (Aldershot, UK: Ashgate, 2002); Kenneth Archer, *A Pentecostal Hermeneutic for the Twenty-First Century: Spirit, Scripture, and Community* (New York: T&T Clark, 2004); Roger Stronstad, *Spirit, Scripture and Theology: A Pentecostal Perspective* (Baguio City, Philippines: Asia Pacific Theological Seminary Press, 1995).

5 Yong, *Spirit-Word-Community*, 138.

6 The various traditions have much to learn from each other, but quite honestly I do not see the scales as entirely balanced since a two-millennia tradition would appear in the natural at least to have more weight than a one- or three- or even five-hundred-year tradition. Please pardon my Catholic bias!

7 James B. Shelton, "The Miracles of Vatican II," lecture, Men of the Upper Room, Church of St. Bernard of Clairvaux, Tulsa, Oklahoma, 2012.

8 Kallistos, Bishop of Diokleia/Timothy Ware, "Tradition and Personal Experience in later Byzantine Theology," *Eastern Churches Review* 3:2 (1970) 131-41.

9 Benedict XVI encourages scholars "to study the relationship between *Mariology and the theology of the word*. . . . Mary is the image of the Church in attentive hearing of the word of God, which took flesh in her. Mary also symbolizes openness to God and others; an active listening which interiorizes and assimilates, one in which the word becomes a way of life." *Verbum domini (On the Word of God in the Life and Mission of the Church)*, Post-Synodal Apostolic Exhortation, September 30, 2010 (Vatican City: Libreria Editrice Vaticana, 2010) §27. Andreas Hoeck says that Peter uses a Marian hermeneutic in his first speech in Acts. The speech demonstrates the apostles' high degree of sensitivity to the scriptural authority, especially that of the ancient prophets. "The Apostolic Speeches in Acts and Seminary Teaching Methods" (paper presented at the Second Quinn Conference, University of St. Thomas at Saint Paul, Minn., June 9–11, 2011) 3.

10 For John Henry Newman, "Mary is our pattern of Faith, both in the reception and in the study of Divine Truth. She does not think it enough to accept, she dwells upon it . . . first believing without reasoning, next from love and reverence, reasoning after believing. And thus she symbolizes to us, not only the faith of the unlearned, but of the doctors of the Church also, who have to investigate, and weigh, and define, as well as to profess the Gospel." "The Theory of Developments in Religious Doctrine," in *Fifteen Sermons Preached before the University of Oxford between A.D. 1826 and 1843* (New York: Longmans, Green, 1900) 313. Sally Cunneen also points out Newman's appreciation of Mary's "reliance on observation and judgment as well as her ability to live with ambivalence." "Breaking Mary's Silence: A Feminist Reflection on Marian Piety," *Theology Today* 56:3 (1999) 323.

11 Bernard Lonergan, *Method in Theology* (Toronto: University of Toronto Press for Lonergan Research Institute of Regis College, 1990).

12 S. Shelton, "Overshadowed by the Spirit."

13 John Henry Newman, *An Essay on the Development of Christian Doctrine* (Notre Dame, Ind.: University of Notre Dame Press, 1989).

14 Bernard Lonergan, *Insight: A Study of Human Understanding,* 5th ed. (Toronto: University of Toronto Press for Lonergan Research Institute of Regis College, 1992).

15 Lonergan, *Insight*, 746.

16 Lonergan, *Method*, 130.

17 René Laurentin calls the different portrayals of Mary given by the biblical authors as a "biblical pluralism . . . [that] can broaden our field of vision . . . [and] lead to an open-minded re-appraisal of a fullness of light transcending the bounds of our individual horizons. The light may come to us through different intermediaries: Paul, Luke, John, but it has only one original source shining through our differing cultures and denominations: the only Holy Spirit." "Pluralism about Mary: Biblical and Contemporary," in *Mary and Ecumenism: Papers of the 1981 International Congress of the Ecumenical Society of the Blessed Virgin Mary*, ed. James Walsh (London: The Way, 1982) 91.

18 Oberman, "Evangelical Perspective," 273.

19 The term "separated brethren" was used in Vatican II's decree on ecumenism to refer to non-Catholic Christians. I use the term here in a reciprocal sense, to refer to

the way both Catholics and non-Catholics tend to view each other. Second Vatican Council, *Unitatis redintegratio,* promulgated by Pope Paul VI, November 21, 1964: http://www.vatican.va/archive/hist_councils/ii_vatican_council/documents/vat-ii_decree_19641121_unitatis-redintegratio_en.html .

20 Lonergan, *Method,* 161.

21 Lonergan, *Method,* 106.

22 Catholic Church, International Theological Commission, "Theology Today: Perspectives, Principles and Criteria," *Origins* 41:40 (March 15, 2012) 641–61; Yong, *Spirit-Word-Community,* 138. Drawing from C. S. Peirce, Yong speaks of the provisional nature of theological propositions as fallibilism: "All theological claims are fallible at worst and partial at best, subject to the ongoing quest driven by the pneumatological imagination. Yong, "The Hermeneutical Trialectic: Notes Toward a Consensual Hermeneutic and Theological Method," *Heythrop Journal* 45 (2004) 33; Yong, "The Demise of Foundationalism and the Retention of Truth: What Evangelicals Can Learn from C. S. Peirce," *Christian Scholar's Review* 29:3 (2000) 570–71. Faith and Order Commission, *A Treasure in Earthen Vessels: An Instrument for an Ecumenical Reflection on Hermeneutics,* Faith and Order Paper, 182 (Geneva: World Council of Churches, 1998) §A2: "Faith also relies upon human forms of expression and interpretation, dialogue and communication, all of which are fragile and all too often fragmented embodiments, none of which is completely adequate, of the mystery which has been revealed. ... Only at the end of time will the Church's contemplation of God's revealed mystery go beyond a partial knowledge and arrive at that 'knowing even as we are known' of which Paul writes in 1 Cor 13:9–12."

23 Balthasar sees Christ as God's own exegesis of himself, i.e., the one who makes God known through the incarnation (John 1:18). The Holy Spirit interprets Christ to humanity in every age in a way that is ever new, yet ever the same. Hans Urs von Balthasar, "God Is His Own Exegete," *Communio* 13:4 (1986) 280–87.

24 Raneiro Cantalamessa, "'Scripture Breathes Forth God': 4th Lenten Sermon of Father Cantalamessa," *Zenit,* March 14, 2008 [6 pp.]. Online http://www.zenit.org/article-22059?l=english. It is this same type of reading to which Francis Martin and Clark Pinnock refer. See, e.g., Martin, "Spirit and Flesh in the Doing of Theology," *Journal of Pentecostal Theology* 18 (2001) 5–31. Pinnock, "The Work of the Holy Spirit in Hermeneutics," *Journal of Pentecostal Theology* 2 (1993) 3–23.

25 Henri de Lubac, *Medieval Exegesis,* vol. 2, *The Four Senses of Scripture,* trans. E. M. Macierowski (Grand Rapids: Eerdmans, 2000) 193.

26 Raneiro Cantalamessa, "Scripture Breathes Forth God."

27 Walter Brueggeman defines hermeneutic as "a proposal for reading reality through a certain lens." "II Kings 18–19: The Legitimacy of a Sectarian Hermeneutic," *Horizons in Biblical Theology* 7:1 (1985) 22. An ecumenical hermeneutic then would be one that can use different lenses as needed.

28 Joseph Ratzinger, later Benedict XVI, describes "the kernel of the New Testament, that is, to what alone justifies the very existence of Christendom" as "faith in truth disclosing itself." "What Unites and Divides Denominations? Ecumenical Reflections," *Communio: International Catholic Review* 1:2 (March—April 1972) 116.

29 Hans Urs von Balthasar warns of "theology at prayer" being superseded by "theology at the desk." "Theology and Sanctity," in his *Explorations in Theology*, vol. 1, *The Word Made Flesh* (San Francisco: Ignatius Press, 1989), 208. Geoffrey Wainwright, *Orthodoxy: The Praise of God in Worship, Doctrine, and Life: A Systematic Theology* (New York: Oxford University Press, 1980) 5.

30 Lonergan, *Insight*, 754–55.

31 Congar, "Conquering," 108–9.

32 Lonergan, *Method*, 122–23.

33 Joseph Ratzinger, "What Unites and Divides Denominations? Ecumenical Reflections," *Communio* 1:2 (1972) 119.

POVERTY REDUCTION AS A CHRISTIAN CALL

A VIEW ON MICROFINANCE LOANS FROM PENTECOSTAL CHURCHES IN ZAMBIA

IRENE BANDA

Spiritus 2.1–2 (2017) 77–98
http://digitalshowcase.oru.edu/spiritus/

Key words *poverty, spirituality, financial services, livelihoods*

Abstract

The impact of microfinance activities in reducing poverty has received mixed reviews. Some studies show positive impact while others show increasing criticism towards practices considered deleterious to poor people's welfare. There are similar opinions amongst Pentecostal churches in Zambia. These churches acknowledge the usefulness of microfinance, but because of negative experiences, they are concerned about its efficacy. The general observation of these churches is that spiritual maturity helps those living in poverty identify the root causes, and are therefore able to plan tangible ways out of poverty. They assert that when people grow spiritually and biblical principles like those in 2 Thessalonians 3:10 are employed, they become more responsible and can use microfinance loans with higher success rates. On the contrary, they observe that poor people who are not grounded spiritually tend to abuse microfinance services by either borrowing more than they need, using loan funds for unintended purposes or generally failing to pay back as agreed. This article presents those views within the context of microfinance provision that responds poor people's needs.[1]

Even while we were with you, we gave you this command:
"Those unwilling to work will not get to eat." Yet we hear that
some of you are living idle lives, refusing to work and meddling
in other people's business. We command such people and urge
them in the name of the Lord Jesus Christ to settle down and
work to earn their own living (2 Thessalonians 3:10–12 NLT).

Microfinance and the Poverty Concern

"*N*ame the problem so we can fix it," so the saying goes. Naming
the root problems that cause poverty has been the subject of intense
debate in the development discourse, without concrete agreement and
therefore no sustainable "fix." Attempts at providing welfare support
are frowned upon as perpetuating poverty and creating dependency.
Furthermore, welfare support is seen as not empowering but rather
reducing people's self-determination. Regardless of these views, microfinance is considered an appropriate response to poverty because it
recognizes poor people's inherent capacity to help themselves.

To demonstrate the positive impact of microfinance, Daley-Harris
tells the story of Saraswathi Krishnan of India. Saraswathi's husband was
an unskilled wage laborer who earned very little and squandered it all
on alcohol.[2] In desperation, following the increasingly depraved state
of their lives, Saraswathi sold her daughter into bonded labor in order
to meet some of the bills. Five years later she joined a women's self-help
group with a microcredit program. Here she got a loan that enabled her
to buy back her daughter and start a small vegetable-selling business.
With progressive loans, her economic status improved and so did her
family's livelihood.

It is evident that many living in poverty like Saraswathi are already
doing micro- and small businesses. However, often they lack access
to financial resources to enable them increase business activities and
incomes in order to address the poverty conundrum. In response to
this need, significant resources have been channeled into microfinance
to enable access to credit by more poor people. Between 2004 and
2006, the global stock of foreign capital investment into microfinance,

covering both debt and equity, more than tripled to US$4 billion.[3] By the end of 2014, it was estimated that investments in microfinance had gone up from US$8.7 million in 2012 to US$10.4 billion.[4] In the 2004 annual report, the Microcredit Campaign reported that 3,164 microfinance institutions had reached 92 million clients, two thirds of whom were rated the poorest. The report further stated that 66.6 million clients impacted 333 million family members as a result of their improved financial status.[5] This significance was firmly endorsed when the United Nations declared 2005 as the International Year of Microcredit and various events were organized that sought to raise the profile of microfinance.[6] Further, in 2006 the Nobel Peace Prize was awarded to Mohammed Younus who is credited with founding modern-day microfinance. The prize was shared with his Grameen Bank, which is a microfinance institution.[7]

However, despite growth in microfinance, critics questioned its efficacy and raised concerns about whether the problem of lack of financing was indeed at the root of poverty. As Christians have engaged with microfinance from the perspective of responding to Christ's call towards social action, it raises the issue of whether there is a biblical view that redefines the poverty problem. In response, this paper will begin by overviewing microfinance and areas of criticism. The paper will provide an analysis of the views of Pentecostal church leaders in Zambia and discuss the biblical view of poverty. In conclusion, it will propose an approach to developing a different process for engaging with poverty reduction strategies that include but are not limited to microfinance.

What Is Microfinance?

The utility value of money is ubiquitous with everyday living, commerce, and trade. It is at the core of general economic development for individuals, families, and nations alike. For money to fulfill these functions, it must be readily available, affordable, and fungible.[8] The basic financial impulse, therefore, is to save for the future, especially because future needs can be unpredictable. However, the availability of money to individuals is tied to their economic well-being, and this puts poor people at a disadvantage because they often do not have readily available money. Thus, poverty manifests itself in their failure to pay for day-to-day needs and essential life-cycle needs, such as education, child-birth, marriage ceremonies, medical emergencies, deaths of loved ones, war, and natural calamities, such as floods and droughts. Sometimes poor people have opportunities to invest in existing or new business ventures or to buy land or other productive assets: but without money, investing is impossible.

As the purveyors of money, banks generally do not find serving poor people a compelling business case. The amount of money that poor people are able to save is often too insignificant to warrant the time and effort needed for a financial service. Similarly, requests for credit are often so small and support such vague business proposi-tions that banks consider assessing such requests a waste of resources. Moreover, poor people who are in business often lack credible and trackable records to demonstrate positive business trends and financial discipline. They show limited entrepreneurial skills, lack assets to secure loans, and often live from hand to mouth. The fleeting nature of their business ventures reflects these facts. Yet for these business owners, these activities would be their sole source of income. Because of all this, microfinance has become relevant.

Where It All Started

The history of microfinance is as eclectic as its development. Early initiatives started with Irish Loan Funds in Ireland in 1720. Other early funds can be traced to Germany, France, India, the Netherlands, and Sweden. All had humble beginnings in community efforts.[9] The momentum of modern-day microfinance is rooted in development thinking and action aimed at spurring economic growth in mostly Asian, African, and Latin American countries that had been left behind economically following the post-war rebuilding of Europe and America. It was understood that the absence of industrial activities, especially in form of manufacturing, was the reason for low employment opportuni-ties, leading to depressed incomes and poverty. This understanding led to concerted efforts to prototype business development for small-scale enterprises such that in the 1960s and 1970s, small-scale industries accounted for over 50% of manufacturing employment in various developing countries.

Claims of increasing poverty levels demanded surveys, some of which were championed by the International Labour Organisation (ILO). One important survey revealed that people living in poverty were already involved in activities that generated income. ILO championed the cause of these activities and in 1972 coined the term "informal sector" to denote the space that was serving the employment needs of small and micro enterprises.[10] The informal sector developed very rapidly. By the 1980s, many of the poorest countries considered the informal sector the right space for development thinking and funding. Micro- and small owner-managed businesses would typically be a woman selling vegetables from her homestead or by the roadside; an individual running an internet café; an artisan producing household furniture; or a small engineering firm dealing in sophisticated gadgets or software. The owners of these microenterprises would typically be more concerned with their own day-to-day survival and therefore mostly classified as poor. However, the identified problem was that these entrepreneurs had minimal or no access to formal credit services to grow their businesses and increase income. In response to this need, the modern day concept of microfinance was born in the 1970s as a poverty reduction strategy.

Mohammed Younus is credited with spurring microfinance activities through his Grameen Bank model. It started in Jobra, a small village in rural Bangladesh. Younus heard of Sufia, a bamboo stool maker who got raw materials on credit from a moneylender and paid back the loan from sale proceeds. What was concerning to Younus was that the moneylender set both the price of the raw material and the price of the finished product, which he bought from Sufia. The profit Sufia made from this transaction was hardly adequate to meet her needs, but there were no other credit options available to Sufia, which may have led to a better profit margin. An ensuing survey in the area revealed that there were forty-two other people in a similar situation. Motivated by this, Younus provided his own money as credit to pay off the money-lenders and finance those businesses. His response marked the beginning of the Grameen Bank.[11]

Through various experiments over time and adaptations over regions, microfinance has evolved specific financial products and methods targeting poor people. For example, clients are attended to in their areas of business, contrary to the traditional requirement that a client visit the bank. Moreover, in order to create efficiencies, accounting systems and software appropriate for microfinance activities developed. Microfinance staff were also trained appropriately.[12] With access to more working capital, some clients were able to purchase stock in bulk and benefit from higher profit margins from retail trading. Others diversified into more lucrative products. Yet others invested in tools and equipment for business development.

Microfinance Criticism

In spite of reported success, critics felt that some benefits were exaggerated and argued that poverty reduced less than microfinance supporters have claimed. In societies where debt is not normally condoned, microfinance debt was viewed as creating unwanted stigma. Critics noted that sometimes communities require other services such as health care and schools more than microfinance, thus negating its efficacy. Critics also noted that the very poor and the rural poor are often excluded from microfinance programs. Further, the decisions of what is good or what works are often made without the input of poor people. Reports indicated that poor people do not favour working in groups but are compelled to do so by microfinance programming. Critics observe that due to lack of clarity on pricing, poor people have little understanding on the effective cost of funds that they borrow. Thus, although microfinance services are more expensive than the norm, this hardly became an issue of contention for poor people. The fact that Jobra, the Bangladeshi village where Muhammed Younus founded the Grameen Bank in the late 1970s, remains trapped in poverty 30 years later is used as evidence that wherever microfinance saturates the poor, poverty remains endemic.[13]

Ethnographic studies revealed cases where microfinance loans resulted in a new form of domination against poor women, whereby the women signed for the loans but men used the money. Studies also show that loans benefit the rural middle-class who can assure high repayments at the expense of the vulnerable poor.[14] A field staff of a microfinance institution shares frustrations in the discussion of one study:

> I am tired of visiting this neighborhood to pressure people. Yes Mrs. P. is responsible for the loan but she is sick and a widow. She has been harassed by women in her group and by me. I try to be very nice to her, but my job depends on good repayment. My clients do not tell me their troubles any more. Now I am a moneylender and I never hear their news…They do not see me as helping them but, as an enemy.[15]

> Poor people also expressed frustrations: "I spend a lot of time now thinking about my neighbors and who will pay back and who might not… Some I don't trust as much as I did. I worry that their choices may mean they cannot pay back their loans when it is time."

> One client in Egypt said, "Group members came to the house of my father where I lived after my husband had died suddenly. They pounded the door until the neighbors heard and demanded he pay the loan back. My father was shamed and asked me to leave."[16]

Microfinance practitioners have responded to these criticisms by instituting checks and balances to protect clients from unethical practices and by advocating that social performance be demonstrated through various indicators. These responses include the *Imp-Act* initiative to ascertain the real poverty reduction impact and the Smart Campaign to *help microfinance institutions focus on their real reason for existence, which is serving poor people.*[17] Notwithstanding, the criticisms have led to persistent inquiry about the efficacy of microfinance, with one survey respondent commenting:

> [T]he industry will face a huge reputational risk with the growing clash between opposing ideology and expectations. Is microfinance primarily about financial inclusion or poverty

alleviation? Is microfinance primarily a business opportunity or a development intervention? Does microfinance really meet both financial and social return expectations? Is it an "either or"? Or has microfinance many faces?[18]

As the debate within the industry rages, it begs an understanding of the poor's perspectives regarding their movements out of poverty and the most appropriate tools to help them do so.

An Understanding of the Perspectives of Poor People

Microfinance works on the assumption that poor people are entrepreneurs who need credit to grow their businesses. The reality is often far from this assumption. Often poor people are mostly looking for the safest means of earning an income. They are averse to risks associated with running a business, which often include "problems, including events, conditions, and people that impair the ability to conduct daily business operations . . . characterized by frequent occurrence, disruption, and idiosyncrasy."[19] Sometimes poor people do not use loans for business because they have "either limited capacity to use investment credit or more pressing needs for [financial] products that support consumption and income smoothing."[20]

Furthermore, in the absence of consistent wages, livelihoods that are based on acquiring income become vulnerable to the process of managing those scarce resources. Zollman and Collins elaborate by saying,

> In the absence of reliable lifetime employment, earning and allocating money are inseparable. . . . Cash flows are erratic and unpredictable. . . . Financial decisions that affect family living standards are small, daily expenditure and savings choices, requiring discipline more than analytical skill . . . financial decisions are relentless, unavoidable, and urgent. . . .[21]

This reality is unlike that of middle- or high-income earners, in which earning money and managing money are separable tasks. The reality of the poor requires responding appropriately to their needs. A study commissioned by the World Bank puts this into perspective:

There are 2.8 billion poverty experts, the poor themselves. Yet the development discourse about poverty has been dominated by the perspectives and expertise of those who are not poor— professionals, politicians and agency officials. . . .

What more can be more important than listening to the poor and working with our partners all over the world to respond to their concerns? . . . We are prepared to hold ourselves account- able, to make effort to try to respond to these voices.[22]

Yet the reality is that the voice of poor people will be compromised even where notional dialogue space is afforded them: poor people often lack the capacity to recognize the root causes of poverty and also often lack the competence to negotiate consequent livelihood solutions. In the midst of these dilemmas, the church and Christian microfinance institutions have embraced microfinance in response to their Christian call to social action.

Microfinance and the Church in Social Transformation

Some churches hailed microfinance as an appropriate solution for moving poor people from dependency to participating in their own development and potentially strengthening the local church. These understand that "by participating in microfinance programs, church members can develop occupational skills and learn financial disci- pline. . . . This strengthens the church by improving the economic situation of its members and by putting them in a better position to tithe or donate their time and resources."[23] Proponents of Christian microfinance recognize that the church is already well integrated in the community with access to community groups. They further observe that churches are trusted by borrowers as institutions that care. They are considered compassionate and seen to operate with integrity, which are important aspects for strong microfinance pro- grams. In this regard, churches are regarded as better placed to reach the poorest of the poor.

In talking about the actions of the church in the development arena, Tsele recognizes that, while the church was prolific in incorporating development projects in education, health, and agricultural sectors within missionary endeavors, other development actors have now occupied the space. He asserts that for the church to strengthen its legitimacy in the development domain, there is "an obligation to demonstrate that the church brings something substantive, and that our commitment is driven by different motives."[24] Christian microfinance institutions face the challenge of defining that substantive difference, which would lead to transformation in the lives of the poor. Getu postulates that this happens through Christian microfinance institutions who serve poor people with financial services that enable transformation, innovation, nurturing, stewardship, partnership, and responsiveness. However, he is quick to acknowledge that more work is required to achieve these ideals.[25]

A View from Pentecostal Churches in Zambia

Zambia has a population of 15.2 million people. According to 2014 World Bank statistics, 74.3% live on under $1.25% a day (34% in urban areas and 80% in rural areas).[26] Given this high poverty prevalence, it is highly likely that Pentecostal churches in Zambia are home to a good number of people living in poverty. It is with this in mind that this study includes views from leaders of eight Pentecostal churches in Zambia, most of which have a network of both urban and rural branches. The interviews also include views from the general secretary of the Evangelical Fellowship of Zambia, the umbrella body for all evangelical churches, including Pentecostal churches. Thus the views generated represent interactions with a wide section of Pentecostal believers. The findings are given below and are organized under indicated thematic headings.

The Role of the Church in Poverty Reduction

Respondents acknowledged that the primary role of the church is to preach the gospel and disciple believers to spiritual maturity, with the goal of enabling them to share their faith in their communities. They also indicated that the church has a responsibility to participate in their members' lives for various reasons and circumstances and see this as part of their wider engagement in society. Most of the situations that they have had to deal with in this regard fall into three categories: Firstly, when members, through unforeseen circumstances fall into financial difficulties. Examples of these include sickness, a death of a church member or the member's family member, or emergencies like floods or droughts that create shocks needing more resource support beyond the norm. Secondly, when the livelihoods of church members show serious vulnerabilities and deprivations associated with poverty. Examples include inability to have decent meals, inability to pay for school fees and school requisites, or even inability to meet medical bills. Thirdly, where the church elects to have specific social and economic engagements in their communities as permanent features of the ministry. These include soup kitchens, orphanages, provision of education and health facilities. Some respondents indicated that they answer to all the three categories, while others one or two of the categories.

As indicated earlier, on one end of the spectrum are churches who advocate that poor people should come out of dependency and take up responsibility for their own lives. They base their engagement on 2 Thess 3:10-12, "those unwilling to work will not get to eat" (NLT). These churches identify the root causes of poverty as lack of faithfulness and sinful practices that need transformation in line with the word of God. On the other end of the spectrum are the churches that have a significant involvement in social action. They feel compelled to intervene in improving livelihoods, because they already have a presence in locations with high incidences of poverty. One such church bases their engagement on Deut 15:7-8 (ESV),

> If among you, one of your brothers should become poor, in any of your towns within your land that the Lord your God has given you, you shall not harden your heart or shut your hand against your poor brother, but you shall open your hand to him and lend him sufficient for his need, whatever it may be.

This dichotomy of churches working at different ends of the spectrum reveals, nonetheless, their shared concern for people living in poverty. Hence, it is necessary to review the problems that lead to poverty as defined by the church leaders and how that understanding has informed the solutions employed.

The Faces of Poverty

Respondents with a firm belief that poor people should take responsibility for their own lives come from an understanding that the root causes of poverty lie in humanity's sinful nature. Their interventions start with an assessment to determine what responsibility or irresponsibility led to a poverty situation in a church member's life, in order to provide appropriate counsel or intervention. They would therefore deal with tragedy differently from the way they would deal with a member who fails to pay school fees. The former would be viewed as more of an unforeseen occurrence and the later as a failure to plan. They believe that as people begin to leave sinful practices, walk in faith, learn generosity, and apply godly wisdom, they will start to make dramatic steps out of poverty. This belief sits on the understanding that root causes of poverty are dealt with as a believer has their mind and heart transformed by the word of God.

The respondents who are significantly involved in poor people's lives observe that poor families often depend on others to help them and the church becomes the first place to go to. Comments from those who took part in the interview attest to a dependency attitude among people living in poverty. Several leaders reiterate this dependency attitude as part of the challenge the church faces in helping the poor. According to one respondent,

> As we were praying for employment for young people, one was offered K5.00[27] and asked to use and multiply it. He laughed that he could not multiply it in a week. He returned the K5.00 after the week saying that there was no business that could use that paltry sum. He was advised to go and buy traditional brooms and resell them. He went and invested the K5.00 into sugarcane and turned the money into K30.00. He managed to raise a further K300.00 and went into banana business. Three months later he was nicely dressed and doing well at home.[28]

This attitude makes it difficult to arrive at sustainable solutions. I encountered this tendency in my recent research with communities and traced its beginnings in Zambia to the days of early industrialization. The industrialization process triggered rural-to-urban migrations in pursuit of mining employment. Employment brought income for livelihoods but at the same time removed the aspect of being inward-looking in the quest for income. People had to look to the employer for their livelihoods and thus began depending on external entities. This process is visualized in the diagram below, which traces the possible origins of dependency in Zambia.

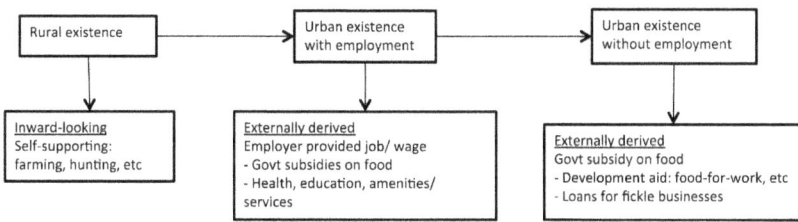

```
┌──────────────────┐        ┌──────────────────┐        ┌──────────────────┐
│ Rural existence  │──────► │ Urban existence  │──────► │ Urban existence  │
│                  │        │ with employment  │        │ without employment│
└──────────────────┘        └──────────────────┘        └──────────────────┘
         │                           │                           │
         ▼                           ▼                           ▼
┌──────────────────┐   ┌──────────────────────────┐   ┌──────────────────────────────┐
│ Inward-looking   │   │ Externally derived       │   │ Externally derived            │
│ Self-supporting: │   │ Employer provided job/   │   │ Govt subsidy on food          │
│ farming, hunting,│   │ wage                     │   │ - Development aid: food-for-  │
│ etc              │   │ - Govt subsidies on food │   │   work, etc                   │
│                  │   │ - Health, education,     │   │ - Loans for fickle businesses │
│                  │   │   amenities/ services    │   │                               │
└──────────────────┘   └──────────────────────────┘   └──────────────────────────────┘
```

Steps towards Solutions

The churches that are active in the lives of poor people explore various ways of helping them including possible business activities. However, they have found that the businesses tend to be fickle and profit margins small. Some churches facilitate training in basic skills in entrepreneurship and seek to encourage agricultural production for the rural congregations. Some encourage their members to form savings groups. To a large extent, the solutions call for money as a key resource. The respondents agree that this is in short supply and that the church is unable to meet poor people's needs. I then inquired if, in their quest for money, they had had any dealings with microfinance and what their experiences were like.

Interactions with Microfinance Organizations

None of the respondents had any direct dealings with microfinance institutions on behalf of their members. A good number, including the Evangelical Fellowship of Zambia, started microfinance activities but quickly realized that it was not working when church members failed to pay back what they owed. In its place, a number of churches started and encouraged formation of savings groups.

The interview sought to find out what respondents think of micro-finance as a poverty reduction strategy. The majority believe that micro-finance does not work well in reducing poverty, although if it is implemented responsibly, it might bring about transformation by utilizing kingdom principles. There was a strong view amongst respondents that they would not refer any of their church members to microfinance institutions, because these institutions would not help members grow. Some respondents feel that microfinance is driven from a western agenda, which views Africa as this massive mess of poverty needing help, and as such does not prioritize preparing poor people to benefit from the intervention. Others believe microfinance perpetuates the narrative that if poor people get money from someone, they would be able to put their life together even without taking time to clarify how this would happen, if at all. This has the potential of portraying the churches that support micro-finance as poor stewards of resources especially when poor people fail to pay or fall even deeper into debt.

The Church Exploring New Frontiers

Pentecostal churches in Zambia recognize that they have a role in the lives of their members beyond preaching. In looking at their interactions with microfinance, it became evident that generating money is important to help people out of depravity and the vulnerabilities that manifest from poverty. However generating money is difficult for various reasons, including the fact that poor people have dependency attitudes that negate efforts to secure long-term solutions. The church also simply does not have the kinds of resources needed to ensure long-term solutions. Even when they do give out the money, they have no way of knowing whether a need is truly met or not. This limitation then raises questions regarding the church's role. There is adequate discomfort among Pentecostal churches regarding the efficacy of microfinance practice to warrant questions regarding whether the root causes of poverty call for microfinance as an appropriate solution.

Furthermore, it is necessary to acknowledge that, although microfinance aims to impact poor people positively, it is a hard goal to attain, given that microfinance managers' primary objectives are skewed towards the needs and demands of their organizations. This means that moving people out of poverty will always take second place. Since it is only those experiencing poverty who can confirm livelihood changes, progressive interventions have to be rooted among them by understanding the underlying problems. This diagram visualizes the phenomenon of microfinance interacting with communities living in poverty.

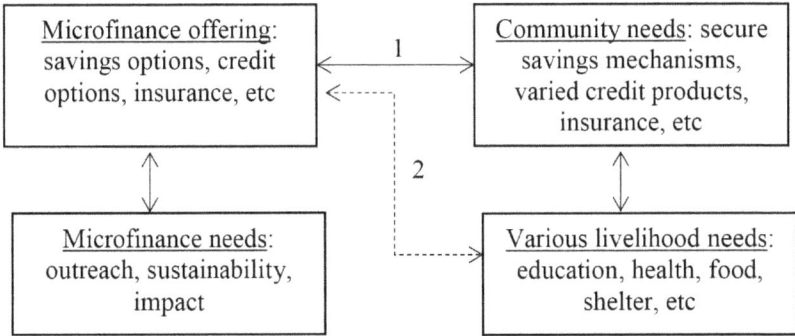

```
┌─────────────────────┐          1          ┌─────────────────────┐
│ Microfinance offering: │ ←─────────────→ │ Community needs: secure │
│ savings options, credit │                   │ savings mechanisms,    │
│ options, insurance, etc │ ←----------┐      │ varied credit products, │
└─────────────────────┘            ┊      │ insurance, etc         │
         ↕                       2  ┊      └─────────────────────┘
                                    ┊                 ↕
┌─────────────────────┐            ┊      ┌─────────────────────┐
│ Microfinance needs:   │            └----→ │ Various livelihood needs: │
│ outreach, sustainability, │                 │ education, health, food, │
│ impact                │                   │ shelter, etc           │
└─────────────────────┘                   └─────────────────────┘
```

The interaction between microfinance institutions and communities, represented by #1, is the first and only line of interaction with the community. Determining livelihood impact would require firstly understanding whether a financial service is addressing the part of the problem that is causing poverty, and then the beneficiary will have to confirm its efficacy. This is represented by #2 (the dotted line) where microfinance institutions do not interact with the community. At this level, the church is active and therefore successful intervention requires exloring the root cause of poverty and locate the perspectives of Pentecostal church leaders. The next section will aim to draw a perspective from the Bible.

Understanding the Root Causes of Poverty: A Biblical View

Bryant L. Myers recognizes that "the nature of poverty is fundamentally relational and its cause is fundamentally spiritual."[29] He notes that by creating humans to be fruitful, to increase in number and fill the earth, and subdue it, God established a common cultural foundation for all human enterprises. He asserts that as stewards of God's resources, humanity has specific responsibilities for sharing resources because all land and natural resources are gifts to all humanity. Myers highlights an interesting argument that the right for all to use the earth's resources predates the right to own, thereby challenging modern-day practices that bestow rights to resources on some people to the exclusion of others.[30]

Another way in which humanity stewards creation is through the responsibility to work. God created humans in his image to work and be productive. Therefore one has a duty to help people work so they can fulfill their purpose. In doing this, another expectation of growth is fulfilled. God's instruction to be fruitful and increase applies to the numerical growth of people, and also to the means to support them. Myers asserts, "God has given humankind the ingenuity and adaptability necessary to create this necessary increase."[31]

The last way humanity is responsible as stewards is by ensuring productivity that they can enjoy. As productive beings, there is an expectation to enjoy the end-product of one's work, which can happen only when people actually produce. As people begin to be productive and enjoy the fruits of their labours, poverty is dealt with.

The creation story ends with the fall, which works against the harmonious relationships that God designed. As a consequence, humans have become the harbinger of "widespread deception, distortion, and domination in all forms of human relationships— with God, within oneself (and family), within the community and between others, and with the environment."[32] These vices permeate the economic, political, and religious systems. As a result, the concept of stewardship is marred and replaced with notions of ownership and subjugation, with justice becoming the domain of the powerful to the detriment of those in poverty. Ultimately, the fall "affirms the radical nature of evil. . . . and should save us from any temptation toward optimistic belief in the ability of government or the free market or our own efforts at human transformation to change reality of the poor in and of themselves."[33] Without divine providence, the fall may have caused the end of the creation and human story.

Myers discusses this divine providence through the mission, death, and resurrection of Jesus Christ. The core of Jesus Christ's mission was to restore the broken and distorted relationship caused by the fall. In his earthly teaching, he commanded his followers, "Love God with all your heart and with all your soul and with all your strength and with all your mind, and love your neighbor as yourself" (Matt 23:26). His death on the cross epitomizes the abandonment of broken relationships, and brings divine forgiveness and redemption from sin. It is also at the cross that powers and principalities were disarmed, thereby dealing a blow to oppressive societal structures and injustice, as God placed Christ in control of all things (Col 2:20; Eph 1:22). The resurrection is the good news of transformation from death to life and is an action only God could author.

The church remains the representation of the ongoing work of God in the world. It is the bearer of the biblical story and Christ's body in the world. Myers states:

> The goal of the biblical story, then, is the reconciliation of all things, on earth and in heaven with Christ as the head. Relationships are restored in all the dimensions distorted by sin—the gospel is the news that distorted patterns of power have been broken; the reception of the gospel is the embrace of radically transformed patterns of social relationships.[34]

What does working with development interventions such as microfinance mean for a church that has embraced an understanding of poverty as described above? The starting point is realizing that Jesus was anointed "to preach good news to the poor . . . to proclaim freedom for the prisoners and recovery of sight for the blind, to release the oppressed, to proclaim the year of the Lord's favor" (Luke 4:18–19). The good news includes a holistic understanding of all human enterprise.

The early church presents a prototype that the modern church can work with. In the early church, the newly Spirit-filled apostles were keen to promote the gospel, but they faced a complaint regarding food distribution. They realized that they could not neglect preaching the word in order to distribute food, yet that was also necessary. They decided to put together a structure managed by Spirit-filled leaders to enable equitable distribution (Acts 6:1–5). Just as the apostles felt the need to prioritize preaching the gospel and to distribute food to needy widows, so the modern church could use a similar approach. The church can do this by setting structures to serve the daily needs of people, while focusing on the core work of ministering the Word. The church is already present in the community with the good news that brings an awareness of sin and its practices, which is at the root of poverty as discussed above. The church can therefore consider community structures that emulate the spirit of Acts 6:1–5.

Creating Community Structures

In order to create empowering community structures, the following elements would need to be considered: context, structure, motive alignment, ability to identify problems, and setting normative standards. The context needs to facilitate the core message of the gospel towards spiritual maturity, which will help bring freedom and create a space for members to articulate their needs. The structure would consist of leaders who show love, empathy, and provide a dependable point of recourse, so that members can know how to handle vexing situations. Motive alignment must be based on godly principles that ensure continuous support to strengthen spiritual maturity in order to impact the community and strengthen others. The ability to identify problems would mean that as people are released from sin's bondage, they would recover their capacity to identify secondary issues affecting livelihoods that would need to be addressed with appropriate solutions for lasting impact. The solutions could include, but not be limited to microfinance. Lastly, setting normative standards would entail determining certain livelihood standards below which action would need to be taken. The following diagram provides a visual for an approach that churches could pursue.

COMMUNITY CONTEXT

- Church leaders focus on Core message of the gospel;
- Spiritual matuiity for responsible individual and collective actions based on Godly principles
- Institute community structure emulating Acts 6 version of community engagement
- Select and appoint mature spirit-filled persons to lead the work ofsocial action in community
- Provide top-lelvel oversight to this structure

Structure:
- Under leadership of mature spirit- flled persons
- Structure providing dependable point of recourse for members
- Leaders that show genuine emphathy and care

Ability to identify problems:
- Release of bondage from sin through spiritual ministry- preaching of gospel
- ensuring adequate competence to identfy root problems in community
- ensuring adequate competence to identify solutions ncluding micro finance
- Ensuring adequate competence to negotiate conditions

Motive-Alignment:
- Based on Godly principles- all look to God.
- Reduced incidences of injustice
- No one taken advantage of others e.g. poor people

Setting normative livelihood standards:
- community should agree on livelihood standards so that no one has to live beyond those standard because action will have been taken.

Measuring Impact

Within this structure, there would be need to ensure that interventions are not only owned by members, but that they build on the spiritual maturity and actually produce impactful outcomes. Thus impact has to be measured within the community, with three elements being essential to ensure progressive outcomes: 1) that interventions are owned by members; 2) that they are built on the spiritual maturity; and 3) that they actually produce impactful outcomes. The process of determining the impact of interventions would be structured to respond to the following questions at the start of the intervention:

What are the livelihood needs? The response at the outset will help determine if the proposed solutions will address the articulated need. When measuring impact, how the livelihood needs were addressed will be an important indicator for effectiveness.

What financial services are needed? This question will help prescribe the type of financial service needed to address the situation. When measuring impact, how the money was used will be an important indicator for the efficacy of the financial service.

How is the need for financial services going to be met? This question will help point to the actual provision of the financial service and understanding the intricate details such cost of funds (interest rates), rules of engagement with the service providers and any other stipulations that would need to be clarified.

In the final analysis, this process should lead to expansive learning for both the community and the various providers of services including microfinance practitioners.

Conclusions

This study recognizes the value and shortfalls of microfinance services. The article analyzes the views of Pentecostal church leaders in Zambia and confirmed the shortcomings of microfinance. The analysis also reveals a spiritual aspect to poverty in locating the root cause of poverty in sinful practices. Since sin is addressed through the mission, death, and resurrection of Christ, with the effect of restoring broken relationships, a means is already in place to adequately manage poverty. The early church in the Book of Acts provides a prototype for addressing human need within the context of preaching the gospel towards spiritual maturity. In this way the church can address poverty from a biblical standpoint.

Irene Banda (Mutalima) (ibamuta@gmail.com) serves as CEO of TUCUZA Associates, Ltd., Lusaka, Zambia.

Notes

1 This study draws on my PhD thesis entitled, "Responding to Poor People's Voices through Microfinance in Sub-Saharan Africa: An Action Research Study in Zimbabwe and Zambia" (a PhD dissertation, Oxford Centre for Mission Studies and Middlesex University, 2016).

2 S. Daley-Harris, *Pathways out of Poverty—Innovations in Microfinance for the Poorest Families* (Sterling, VA: Kumarian, 2002).

3 X. Reille and S. Forster, "Foreign Capital Investment in Microfinance Balancing Social and Financial Returns" (Consultative Group for Assisting the Poorest Focus Note #44, February 2008).

4 Symbiotics Group, "Symbiotics Microfinance Investments Vehicles Survey: A Study of Global Microfinance Investment Funds," 9th ed. (http://www.syminvest.com/papers/b3e10003-6c18-4126-94fe-8f837523e332, 2015), accessed Oct. 12, 2015.

5 S. Davis and Y. Khosla, Y. 2006: "Taking Stock of the Microcredit Summit Campaign" (www.microcreditsummit.org/papers/Assocsession/DavisKhosla.pdf0 2015), accessed Feb. 22, 2011.

6 United Nations, 2004- "UN Launches International Year of Microcredit 2005" (http://www.un.org/press/en/2004/dev2492.doc.htm, 2004), accessed March 5, 2016.

7 T. Dichter, "Introduction," in T. Dichter and M. Harper, eds., *What's Wrong with Microfinance?* (Intermediate Technology Publications, 2007) 1.

8 Being fungible means that money meant for one purpose can easily be used for a different purpose.

9 H. D. Seibel, "Does History Matter? The Old and The New World of Microfinance in Europe and Asia" (www.econstor.eu/dspace/bitstream/10419/23654/1/2005-10_The_Old_and_the_New_World_in_Europe_and_Asia.pdf , 2005), accessed May 4, 2017.

10 Dichter, "Introduction," 3.

11 A. Dowla and D. Barua, *The Poor Always Pay Back: The Grameen II Story* (Sterling, VA: Kumarian Press, 2006).

12 Dichter, "Introduction," 3.

13 M. Bateman, 2011 "Evidence Emerges of a Failed Model," *(http://indiamicrofinance.com/evidence-emerges-failed-model.html),* accessed May 4, 2017.

14 L. Karim, *Microfinance and its Discontents: Women in Debt in Bangladesh* (Minneapolis: University of Minnesota Press, 2011).

15 K. Wilson, "The Moneylenders' Dilemma" in *What's Wrong with Microfinance?* Eds. T. Dichter & M. Harper (Intermediate Technology Publications, UK) 103.

16 Ibid. 103

17 SMART Campaign, "The Client Protection Principles" (www.smartcampaign.org/about-the-campaign, 2011), accessed June 2, 2011.

18 D. Lascelles and S. Mendelson, 2011: "Microfinance Banana Skins 2011: Losing Its Fairy Dust?" *Financial World* Number 99 (February, 2011) 22.

19 B. DeBerry and E. A. Elliot, "African Microentrepreneurship: The Reality of Everyday Challenges," *Journal of Business Research* 65 (December, 2012) 1666.

20 J. Ledgerwood and A. Gibson, "The Evolving Financial Landscape," in *The New Microfinance Handbook: A Financial Market System Perspective* (Washington, DC: World Bank, 2012) 15.

21 J. Zollmann and D. Collins, D. 2010- "Financial Capability and the Poor: Are We Missing the Mark?" *FSD Insights* 2 (www.fsdkenya.org/insights/10-12-14_Financial_Capability_&_the_Poor_Methodology.pdf, 2010), accessed March 25, 2015.

22 D. Narayan, R. Chambers, M. K. Shah, and P. Petesch, *Voices of the Poor Crying Out for Change* (Washington, DC: World Bank; and Oxford: Oxford University Press, 2000) 2.

23 M. C. Boucher, "Ten Talents: The Role of Church-based Programs in the Microfinance Industry," *Missiology: An International Review* 40:2 (2012) 170.

24 M. Tsele, "The Role of the Christian Faith in Development," in D. Belshaw, R. Calderisi, and C. Sugden, eds., *Faith in Development: Partnership Between the World Bank and the Churches of Africa* (Washington, DC: World Bank; Oxford: Regnum Books, 2001) 209.

25 M. Getu, "Microfinance Criticism and Christian Response," M. Getu, ed., *Transforming Microfinance: A Christian Approach* (Oxford: Regnum Books, 2013) 239.

26 United Nations Development Plan, Lusaka, "Zambian Human Development Report 2016" (http://hdr.undp.org/sites/default/files/zambia_human_development_report_2016.pdf), accessed May 4, 2017.

27 K10.00 for US$1 is used as an indicative rate.

28 Interview with Senior Pastor, Antioch Bible Church, Kitwe, Zambia, January 26, 2017.

29 B. L. Myers, *Walking with the Poor: Principles and Practices of Transformational Development* (Maryknoll, NY: Orbis, 1999) 13.

30 Myers, *Walking with the Poor*, 26

31 Myers, *Walking with the Poor*, 27

32 Myers, *Walking with the Poor*, 27

33 Myers, *Walking with the Poor*, 30

34 Myers, *Walking with the Poor*, 42

THE GOOD LIFE
DESCRIPTORS OF CHANGE IN ROMA PENTECOSTAL COMMUNITIES IN SERBIA AND CROATIA

MELODY J. WACHSMUTH

Spiritus 2.1–2 (2017) 99–118
http://digitalshowcase.oru.edu/spiritus/

Key Words *Roma, Gypsy, Pentecostalism, transformation, identity, reconciliation, Croatia, Serbia*

Abstract

Studies in specific geographical contexts have shown that the spread of Pentecostalism's influence on Roma communities is twofold: it is linked to social change, including a rise of education levels, literacy, decrease in crime, better relationships with the majority culture; and it is also instrumental in the fostering of a "trans-national" identity and revitalization of their respective Roma identities. However, Pentecostalism cannot be considered a formula that intersects with a Romani community with consequential predictable results— in fact, in Southeastern Europe, Romani Pentecostalism is growing at a much slower rate than that of its counterparts in Western Europe and in places such as Romania and Bulgaria. Further, in the language of researchers, NGOs, and the European Union, success is often measured in the appropriated terms of neo-liberal vocabulary: integration, development, and modernization.

In view of these circumstances, through what lens and with whose vocabulary should change and transformation be understood and measured? This paper discusses both the ideal and the current reality of change in Roma communities through the voices of Roma Pentecostal leaders in Croatia and Serbia—with the aim of defining human flourishing and change through the perspective of the Roma.

Introduction

$\mathcal{P}$entecostalism in Roma and Gypsy[1] communities in Europe began in the 1950s and 1960s in places such as France, Spain, Bulgaria, and Romania. Within the last twenty-five years it spread into countries in Southeastern Europe—namely Croatia, Bosnia and Herzegovina, Serbia, Macedonia, Kosovo, Montenegro, Albania and Greece, which have smaller and newer churches. A study on Romani Pentecostalism named it as one of the "foremost religious orientations amongst Roma in Europe and beyond." Although the Roma in Europe are Catholic, Orthodox, Protestant, and Muslim, based on the rates of conversion, Pentecostalism among the Roma will soon outgrow adherents to other Christian traditions and other religions.[2]

The story of Roma Pentecostalism cannot be explored without the larger context—the long and complex history of the Romani and related groups in Europe. Although there are historical accounts of the Roma having a symbiotic relationship with the surrounding cultures—their trades valued as needed skills—there is historical evidence for ill feeling toward the Roma in Central and Eastern Europe by the sixteenth century, with a view of them as "alien" or "other."[3] Under the auspices of various empires, the controlling powers tried to force Roma populations to fit into the mainstream of societies—at best through forced assimilation and at worst through violent means including enslavement and death, culminating in the targeted extermination of Roma during the World War II.[4] Today, although there are a percentage of Roma active in all levels of political, social, and professional engagement, it remains far too small of a percentage in the estimated ten to twelve million Roma in Europe. Particularly in Eastern Europe, the majority of Roma groups retain higher levels of poverty, lower education levels, and higher unemployment than the surrounding majority societies. In addition, deeply embedded stereotypes still largely shape cultural attitudes.[5]

However, speaking about the Roma as a monolithic entity is problematic in any sense, because it ignores the heterogeneous realities of Roma groups existing in different contexts.[6] In terms of Pentecostal research, this is also true—one cannot explore the growth of Roma Pentecostalism without careful attention to context, different emphases, and themes. Therefore, the central question, "How is Pentecostalism impacting Roma communities?" must be explored in specific areas, but in dialogue with the larger context of Roma Pentecostalism. In view of Roma history, careful attention must be paid regarding one's epistemological framework for research. Is it driven by a questionable concept of "ethno-national homogeneity" in Europe's nation states?[7] Is it measured by a neo-liberal development agenda?

Approaching this question requires contextual studies of Roma perspectives on identity, mission, and their place in the global church, since opinions will vary according to regions, countries, or Roma groups. By understanding their vocabulary of change and transformation in conversation with both the wider research on Roma Pentecostalism and missiological studies, Roma Christians can contribute to global Christianity in a unique and significant way. This study draws from current anthropological, sociological, and missiological studies on Roma Pentecostalism to present themes from various contexts. Drawing from five years of primary research including participant-observation, interviews, and informal conversations, this study presents leadership perspectives from Croatia and Serbia. With the view of describing human flourishing and change through the voices of Roma Pentecostal leaders in Croatia and Serbia, their vision will then be discussed in light of current realities.

Overview of Roma Pentecostalism

History and Impact

Roma Pentecostalism first made its appearance in France in the 1950s at a time when countries in Europe were still rebuilding from the previous decades, both materially and spiritually. At that time, the memories of concentration camps for many Gypsies were very fresh.[8] In the same period, a "Gypsy Awakening" began in France after a healing and conversion of a Manouche family. Under the leadership of Clément Le Cossec, it eventually spread to different Roma groups or tribes. Le Cossec began the Gypsy Evangelical Mission (also known as Vie et Lumière). Roma leaders were trained, missionaries were sent out, and key advocates were found in different countries so that these "movements" spread to fifty countries in fifty years. This movement has a large international reach—a branch of the International Light and Life Mission is the Gypsies and Travelers International Evangelical Fellowship (GATIEF), which works in twenty-four countries in America, Asia, Australia, and Europe. [9]

When the French Romani missionaries arrived in the United States in the 1970s, they found that there was already a movement of English Romanichal Pentecostals. In the 1970s and 1980s, churches were planted that were chiefly Romani in membership. [10] In Bulgaria during the 1940s and 1950s, Pentecostalism spread slowly, but after 1989 in both Bulgaria and Romania, rapid growth took place. [11] This is not a uniform movement, but rather "movements." Exact numbers in many locations are hard to come by, but in places like France and Spain, Roma Christians number at least over a hundred thousand (in Spain, over 200,000). [12] In places like Romania and Bulgaria, Roma Christians number in the tens of thousands; in Hungary and Slovakia, in the thousands. Some of the movements are completely independent—having their own theological and mission training schools, while others are under the umbrella of denominations within the country. To make the story more complicated, with the growing economic crisis in places such as Romania and Bulgaria, Roma have traversed over to Western Europe looking for work and started their own churches in places such as England and Germany. [13]

Sociological and anthropological studies in specific geographical contexts have shown that the spread of Pentecostalism in Roma communities can affect multiple areas. It is linked to social change ranging from a rise of education levels and literacy to a decrease in crime and domestic violence and an increase in the status of women, and better relationships with the majority culture. It can also contribute to the fostering of a shared identity (across group/tribal lines) and restoration of pride in their Roma identity. [14]

There is a substantial lack of research on Roma Christianity in the disciplines of religious studies or global Pentecostalism. However,

Atanasov's 2008 PhD thesis concludes that amidst Bulgaria's unraveling socio-economic situation, Gypsy Pentecostalism is resulting in the revitalization of individuals, families, and communities in various degrees: "This has been evidenced by the raising of moral standards, deliverance from addictions, lower crime rates, better education, more honesty in business, more opportunities for employment—a significant social lift."[15]

Why Pentecostalism?

Research on Roma Pentecostalism has grown considerably in the last decade. Early studies, such as Patrick Williams' on French Gypsy Pentecostalism in the 1990s, identified conversion to Pentecostalism as a move toward autonomy—adopting the "values" of the *gadje* (non-Roma) under the guise of religion preserved their autonomy. In addition, he understood it as an outcome of urbanization—and also a remedy to drug addiction, violence, and alcoholism.[16] Since this early study, other perspectives have emerged. For example, Pentecostalism is seen as a means of empowerment.[17] In Štěpán Ripka's study on Roma Pentecostalism in Czech Republic and Slovakia, he notes that this empowerment is for Roma to "change their values" and "participate in society," but not to fight the prejudice, discrimination, and oppression.[18] However, he may have narrowly defined what "fighting prejudice" looks like. Some Roma pastors feel that the majority culture must first see the change in Roma individuals and communities, and then the relationship will change.[19] Acton claims it is actually a new way of engaging with state authorities, since its authority lies outside the state.[20]

Deprivation theories have been used to describe the rise of Pentecostal movements, focusing on the link with poverty, migration, and racial segregation.[21] Podolinska's substantial research on Roma Pentecostalism in Slovakia argues against this view, saying that deprivation theory is incomplete. The religiosity of Roma prior to conversion is complementary to Pentecostal praxis, and "identity-construction and the motivation for fulfilling spiritual needs" should warrant as much consideration as the notion that Pentecostalism is filling in the gaps caused by ethnic and socio-economic marginalization.[22] In fact, Cantón-Delgado's research in Spain shows that conversion is higher among the less-marginal groups.[23]

Another view is that Pentecostalism results in the revitalization of identity, considering this faith either as an effective "vehicle of Romani ethnic identity" or as a "new kind of diaspora," resulting from a new belonging in God's family.[24] Many testimonies recount the acceptance of God's love which was transformative. Embracing an identity as a son or daughter of God has replaced a sense of shame with pride and dignity.[25] On the other side, in some contexts, ethnic distinction is still preserved between different Roma groups and between the *gadje* and Roma.[26]

Although this is not emphasized in the literature, my research conducted relates how miraculous healings, visions and dreams play a significant role in the growth of Pentecostalism. This can be seen both on an individual as well as on the corporate level, which in turn becomes a catalyst for widespread revival. Pentecostal Roma pastors argue that the emotive nature of Pentecostalism is important, connecting with the people on a deep level.

Indeed, if anything, this brief summary of Roma Pentecostalism illustrates that it cannot be considered a formula intersecting a community with consequential predictable results. Studying different contexts and diverse perspectives reveals the Roma as a "complex set of communities that challenge the hegemony of categorizing people into ethnicities" and the spread of Pentecostalism as a "number of different revivals" rather than a single story.[27] Pastors and individuals differ on numerous points: their opinion and relationship to the *gadje*, their attitude toward other Roma groups, their concept of mission and church, language usage in church, strict gender codes such as female head coverings, and the issue of dancing in church. Yet such differences should not mute the fact that in the last fifty years, a "discourse has emerged with its own parameters, which is greater than any one particular embodiment of it and its leaders are aware of this."[28]

Roma and Pentecostalism in Southeastern Europe

Socio-economic Context

Southeastern Europe is a context which has often struggled against the control of mighty powers, been subject to numerous wars in the twentieth century, and is currently besieged with political and economic problems. Many Roma in Croatia and Serbia talk fondly of former Yugoslavia, because they generally experienced greater economic and social security. Like other Yugoslavians, most Roma had steady jobs or ways of making income. However, this could be not sustained after the collapse of state socialism, and many Roma did not have the education or higher job skills to pursue other options. Today in Apatin, Serbia, for example, interviewed Roma contrasted their previous work in the factories to their current one: eight hours of physical field labor earning the equivalent of $8.50 a day, collecting scrap metal to sell, or their own small business such as buying and selling chickens.[29]

The Roma were not primarily in the political conversation of the European Union (EU) until the 1990s. Even then, until 2000, the conversation was mainly about their westward movement from Eastern Europe. At that point, the focus shifted to their rights as a minority in their home countries, and this became a "conditional requirement for achieving the ultimate goal of EU membership."[30] Southeastern Europe has participated in several large-scale EU and non-EU projects concerning the Roma. This included the Decade of Roma Inclusion (2005-15), which targeted the areas of education, employment, and health and housing. In 2011, the EU Framework for National Roma Integration Strategies up to 2020 was adopted.

Progress reports from these initiatives have been grim, however, even in the midst of the general socio-economic crisis experienced by the Western Balkans. In fact, recent studies indicate that, despite decades of the EU working towards improving infrastructures, "the overall picture is still bleak and the Roma populations in the Western Balkans continue to face discrimination in almost all spheres of life."[31] A substantial percentage of Roma in the Western Balkans live in deep poverty, facing lack of education, social protection, health, housing and employment. The poverty rate is 36 percent, as compared to 11 percent among non-Roma.[32] In other words, there is a marked difference between the programs, legislation, and language at a higher state and political level in contrast to the reality in the communities themselves. The EU can *disseminate* its norms as a precondition to membership, but these have not shown to actually transform the situation at a grass-roots level.[33]

Religious Context

Pentecostalism in Croatia, Serbia, Bosnia and Herzegovina, Macedonia, Kosovo, and Montenegro does not have big movements and large churches as compared to elsewhere, even with neighboring Romania. Most Croatians would identify as Catholics, and most Serbians would identify as Orthodox. Particularly after the wars in the 1990s, national identity is tightly intertwined with religious identity. Consequently, often evangelical churches such as Baptists and Pentecostals are considered sects by the dominant church traditions. For Croatians and Serbians, evangelical churches are small and slow growing.

The exception to this was a revival in a Roma community that began in Leskovac, Serbia. In the 1970s, Serbian Pentecostal pastor Mio Stanković prayed for a Roma woman who was healed. This reoriented his perspective to begin a "mission-within-a-mission" to the Roma in his Serbian majority church. During the late 1980s and early 1990s, a sudden outpouring of healings and miracles caused a growing number of Roma to come to church for prayer and healing. By the mid-1990s, one meeting multiplied to three in a day to accommodate all the people. The church split in 2005, and at that time it had grown to 1000 people—one tenth of the total Roma population of the city. In the late 1990s, in partnership with an organization from England, the church began to train church planters, and seven churches were planted throughout Serbia. Although not all the church plants succeeded, the movement continues to grow. In 2015, it was estimated that there were eight larger churches and eight house groups of 20–40 people each. In addition, as of 2017, there are several other Roma Pentecostal churches and home groups unaffiliated with this particular movement in Serbia.[34]

Croatia has not seen this kind of rapid growth, but in 2010, leaders from Leskovac visited and encouraged a Roma couple in Eastern Croatia to move forward with their vision to minister to their people. Like Leskovac, a woman's healing was instrumental in forming relationships within the Roma villages in Darda, Croatia, and the couple planted the first Roma church in the fall of 2012. The church remains small (around 30 adults), but has become more multicultural including several Croatians, Dutch, and Americans, although the majority is Roma.

Roma Leaders on Human Flourishing or "The Good Life"

As part of my research, a series of short questions were asked of ten Roma church leaders in Croatia and Serbia from both urban and rural areas.[35] Even from such a relatively small area, interpretations of being Pentecostal varied. One claimed that it was because of the gifts of the Spirit, it "would be hard for a Roma to be Baptist." Another group of leaders said that Pentecostalism is a good fit for Roma because they are very open to the spiritual world. Another emphasized the importance of the role of the Holy Spirit. Yet, another said he was just evangelical, despite a beliefs and praxis usually associated with Pentecostalism. One remarked it was because the gospel came to him through the Pentecostal church: "If I was converted in the Baptist church, I would be Baptist. I am not connected to Pentecostals or anyone else, but connected to Christ."

The central questions were these:

1. How would you describe "shalom" or "a good life" in a Roma context in Serbia or Croatia?

2. How do you define 'change" in an individual and in a community?

3. What things in a Roma community need to change for this to happen?

4. What, if any, is the church's role in helping the relationship between Serbians and Croatians and Roma? Has this improved in your community?

All agreed that nothing is possible without God's initiative, that God changes the person, not organizations, programs, or the EU. One interviewee put it this way:

When the person is changed, they change their surroundings. When God changed me, then through me he changed my family . . . our opinions, customs, etc. When we accept Jesus, Jesus is the one who says what to do. We don't need to tell people what to do . . . how to dress, how to talk, etc.[36]

The Good Life in a Roma Context

When pressed to describe this change, especially what a "good life" would be, the responses varied, albeit with certain common themes.[37] Z. Bakić described change in the areas of "speech, way of life, [and] way of acting." He says that God changed his own perception of life, work, and marriage. Đ. Nikolić pictured a "Roma neighborhood" that would no longer be as typically expected, but would be a "normal" street. The Roma would now be considered as the other national minorities in Croatia, living according to the rules of society, having good relationships with neighbors. He remarked, "I think we need to adjust to Croatians," although his wife vehemently disagreed, arguing that actually far more Croatians were guilty of similar things, but were not subject to a social stigma.

B. Nikolić spoke of decent housing, proper homes with water and electricity so that the kids could go to school clean. The theme emerged of having skills to participate in modern life. Subotin said, "We need to enter modern times and not live like 200 years ago." He went on to describe the good life as "pride in earning one's own income, good health, good relationships with non-Roma."

Raimović, Š. Bakić, Vladica, and Kamberović agreed that the good life would mean change on several fronts.

- Socio-economic: Decline in criminal activity, increase in education, birth of businesses, increase in reading, and integration with other nationalities;

- Family: Mutual respect in the families, peace and patience, decrease of abortions, and women's equality respected;

- Spirituality and Church: Pastors discipling next generation, spiritual growth, more prayer, growing general awareness and changes of worldview.

What, Then, Needs to Change?

Several themes have emerged in the process of field research. For example, education of both adults and children is a prominent theme.

A community leader spoke that part of the challenge is helping the Roma community to accept that education can improve the life of people in the community.[38] A pastor related that recently his own son was not doing well in school. Thus, he took him to visit some very poor Roma families who work constantly to barely eke out a living. "Do you want to do this your whole life?" he asked his son. B. Nikolić spoke about the challenging slow rate of improvement in attitude among girls and young women in the community, with whom she was working for the past five years. "In church, we have about twenty girls who are in school, but only three are going to high school. It is not a drastic change, but God is slowly changing things." Subotin related the steady change in his community where more value is now placed on education: "Eighty percent of youth are now in high school and starting to think more about the future. Beginning to feel less shame, their parents are proud that their children are getting a diploma. This is something new." Many expressed their desire to see Roma occupy influential positions in society as lawyers, doctors, politicians, and educators, and not just the lowest paid jobs in society.

This relates to the critique of "mindset" which many leaders referred to. How would this critique be manifested in everyday life? The first is moving from a day-to-day focus to one taking the future seriously. This relates to all areas from health (preventive health measures vs. emergency) to spending or saving one's paycheck or social help. The second is the creation of awareness within the people themselves about what needs to change in order to be good neighbors. For example, one pastor said, "Educate them on other ways of living. Show them pictures of different ways of living so they can recognize having a garden in the yard instead of disorganized piles of scrap metal to sort and sell for income." The third is demonstrating true change by showing love to each other, giving to others generously, and looking at life positively. The fourth is discouraging the tendency toward early marriage, as Đ. Nikolić said, "I wish more pastors would speak out against this." There are other specific things related to "entering modern society," such as helping people complete their personal documents, legalizing houses, receiving health education, more adults going to school to read and write, and encouraging women's rights. There has also been an emphasis on economic uplift: fighting poverty with more employment and encouraging more entrepreneurship.

Discussion

According to Cantón-Delgado, it is easy to frame the interpretation of Roma Pentecostalism through language that adheres to the goals of the state, studying it only in terms of "integration" or "social benefits." Roma Pentecostalism, she argues, represents "the expression of a non-secular process that can bring (and is in fact bringing) alternative forms of political/cultural affirmation through unexpected ways."[39] For example, in Northern Europe and in England in the nineteenth and early twentieth centuries, spreading Christianity and morality among the Roma was linked to initiatives such as sedenterization, and "reforming the Gypsies" to make them useful citizens. These impulses led to attempts to "purge" children from their Gypsy culture by separating them from their parents into charity schools and forbidding the speaking of Romani.[40]

This "cultural affirmation" through an experiential acceptance of God's love is a key element in terms of holistic transformation. Roma in Croatia and Serbia tend to be more open to spiritual conversations and the spiritual world in general than the majority cultures around them. It is not unusual to hear about a vision or dream, the interpretation of which is often received as a message from God.[41] Church leaders concede, however, that growth and change is slow and tedious. This is expressed by Z. Bakić, "I have been here for twelve years and change is slow. People will convert and [be] baptized, but the change is slow. People are not yet ready for leadership." In Leskovac, the significant changes emerged slowly after three decades. They include a reduction in crime, fewer young marriages, a higher percentage of kids going to high school, decreasing domestic violence and fights between households, and better relationships with the Serbian authorities.

In Croatia, Đ. Nikolić feels overwhelmed with the complexity of problems and questions how he can have influence: "I never did, but now I must think about these things. I see them as a huge problem and I feel very small to do anything about it." This response is understandable due to the layers of social, economic, cultural, and political complexity. The Roma "have been forced to occupy marginal spaces on the fringes of the dominant social and economic systems" and, therefore, developed "the craft of living under the conditions of resource scarcity."[42] This may sometimes mean doing something against the law. For example, suppose that a household, living in sub-standard conditions, is stealing electricity in order to have light. The church cannot merely state that "this is a sin" without addressing the situation around it.

Because of this ongoing complex reality, Roma Pentecostalism cannot be viewed apart from its relationship with its wider social context. In reality, in spite of the vision and desire of most Roma leaders for holistic transformation in their communities, the extent of transformation is correlated to the wider population. In other words, a change can progress only so far before hitting a "glass ceiling" of restrictive attitudes by the majority.[43] These attitudes can either surface blatantly or lurk in subtle forms, shaping non-verbal responses and general orientation.

In the same survey all the leaders except two[44] claim that very little improvement has been made in the relationship between Roma and the majority culture, and this is both a measure of the "good life" as well as a barrier preventing the "good life." In fact, they are keenly aware that discrimination they face is not only from society but also from the wider church. "Although all cultures do bad things, we are sealed forever with certain stereotypes," Đ. Nikolić said. He made a specific reference to the connection always made between Roma and witchcraft. Subotin's social action towards both Serbians and Roma is well known by the municipality in which he lives. Therefore, the authorities support his projects. In the other communities in which he works, things are much more difficult because they do not know him. Recently, he tried to take a group of couples out for dinner as part of a church-sponsored marriage course, but they were refused service from two restaurants as soon as they walked in.

Sometimes it may be fear, based on past experiences or expectation of prejudice, which prevents someone from interacting with the majority culture.[45] For example, B. Nikolić was recently trying to facilitate prayers for all the nations in a children's Sunday school. They reacted strongly against this idea, because, they said, people are always cursing them for being "gypsies." Thus, they did not want to pray for them.[46] That being said, facing fear or expectation of prejudice is much more daunting if one is in a harshly vulnerable position in society.

In addition, as referred to in the earlier literature, Christian Roma can also have an attitude of ethnocentrism toward other Roma groups and the non-Roma. The fear and prejudice on all sides is a serious barrier to transformative mission: "For both the Roma and the *gadje*, these perceptions, assumptions, constructed images, and certainly racism erect complex, mutually reinforcing barriers of isolation and separation that present a serious challenge to the church's participation in God's mission in Central and Eastern Europe."[47]

The church plays a key role in facilitating transformative relationships and community development, and this role is recognized even by non-religious authorities. The two churches in Leskovac both relate how the government recognizes the changes in the surrounding Roma communities and the influence of the churches. As a consequence, they began to consult with the churches and their leaders regarding various issues concerning the Roma. Alijević told of a turning point when he and a Roma civic leader met the Serbian mayor. According to him, "The mayor said that whatever is the need concerning the Roma people, he would consult with me [pastor] rather than the Roma leader, because the people will more likely listen to me." Đ. Nikolić states, "We need to break our prejudices first and change ourselves, not our neighbors . . . but there needs to be some life together, common life together. It is necessary that people trust each other."

The leaders from Croatia and Serbia (as well as other of Southeastern Europe) desire that their church is not just for Roma. Alijević notes, "It is not good to look on who is Roma, Serbian and Croat, because God's word is the same for all. . . . We have a very good fellowship with our Serbian brothers and sisters, and sometimes non-Roma are serving in our church." Further, many hold the idea that God intends to use the Roma to bless the other nations. The three-year-old grassroots movement, Roma Networks, connects Roma leaders and ministries from around Europe. Its common refrain has become "Roma for the nations." Academic studies have described such an impulse as "symbolic inversion of persecution."[48] This concept is nothing new in the biblical narrative and missiological conceptual paradigms, the "least" becoming the catalyst and showcase of God's power and mission taking place from the margins.

Significantly, the founding board of Roma Networks includes a Roma pastor from Serbia and a Croatian woman who serves in a Roma church in Croatia. Their vision of transforming Roma communities emphasizes, among other things, God's reign over ministry territorialism and reconciliation between Roma and non-Roma. The most recent conference in March 2017 highlighted the importance of unity as a witness for the gospel. If this kind of missional vision grows along with the number of Roma Christians in Southeastern Europe, albeit slowly, modeling reconciliation as a paradigm for mission may well serve as the most compelling witness of the gospel to all the nationalities in the region.[49]

Conclusion

In light of the slow growth of Roma Pentecostalism in these countries of Southeastern Europe, set amidst the challenging socio-economic and cultural realities, Roma leaders speak of both the needs and potential for ministry as part and parcel of their view of transformation. There is a spoken need for both missionaries and tools that can speak to the multivalent community issues and train new leaders, as the needs far outweigh the workers. This spoken need, however, has its own challenges, even as in the last ten years, the Roma have become a more popular mission field for Western organizations. One pastor recently spoke of the growing problem of organizations offering money and resources without proper investigation or relationships. Such mission practices, based on the organization's agenda rather than on felt needs, create dependencies, jealousies, and bad practices.[50] Sometimes, Roma leaders feel that their communities and people are used as pictures and headlines to gain financial support or prestige for another organization.

Even good intentions can hide a paternalistic stance of "what needs to happen to fix the community." This orientation is not really different from centuries of attempts to force the Roma into complying with the "symbolic image of how 'proper citizens' should organize their social and economic affairs."[51] In terms of mission, knowledge of this complex history as well as the past mission legacy of "Christianizing and civilizing" in cross-cultural exchanges is critical.

In other words, an awareness of both language and framework for the concept of mission and transformation is important. Schreiter argues that the "ministry of reconciliation is a spirituality rather than a strategy."[52] In an intensely relational Roma context, a spirituality of reconciliation grows most naturally in the soil of constant relationships over time. Roma Pentecostalism in Southeastern Europe is really just beginning. How the global church engages with some of these considerations could determine how it will influence and be influenced by this phenomena.

Melody J. Wachsmuth (mjwachsmuth@yahoo.com) has served as a mission researcerh and writer in Southeastern Europe since 2011. She also serves as a church leader in a Roma majority church in Croatia and is currently a PhD candidate with the Oxford Centre for Mission Studies, studying Roma Pentecostalism in Croatia and Serbia.

Notes

1 The groups of people I intend to refer to when I use "Roma" (which has been adopted for public discourse after 1989) can differ according to how people understand boundaries and markers of identity. These groups of people can be quite diverse, and may differ according to country and context. Sometimes, the way a certain group identifies itself is at odds with how the majority culture or even how academics identify them. Romani people are thought of as an ethnic group with their own language, while Gypsies may be Romani or a related ethnic group including Gypsies, Roma, Sinti, "travellers," Gitano, Dom, Lom, etc. In this paper, I use Roma (and sometimes Gypsy when the historical context requires it) in the broadest sense, to refer to groups possessing related sociological indicators (which may include language, a shared experience, shared sense of history, some common culture) and/or who self-identify as Roma, Romani, or Gypsy. David Thurfjell and

Adrian Marsh, eds., *Romani Pentecostalism: Gypsies and Charismatic Christianity* (New York: Peter Lang, 2014) 8.

2 David Thurfjell and Adrian Marsh, "Introduction," in Thurfjell and Marsh, *Romani Pentecostalism*, 7.

3 David Crowe, *A History of the Gypsies of Eastern Europe and Russia* (New York: Palgrave Macmillan, 2007) xvii, xviii, 35.

4 Elena Marushiakova and Vesselin Popov, "Historical and Ethnographic Background:Gypsies, Roma and Sinti," in Will Guy, ed., *Between Past and Future: The Roma of Central and Eastern Europe* (Hatfield, UK: University of Hertfordshire Press, 2001) 33–53.

5 Štěpán Ripka, "Pentecostalism among Czech and Slovak Roma: The Religiosity of Roma and the Practices of Inclusion of the Roma in the Brotherhood in Salvation, Autonomy and Conversions among Roma in Márov" (a PhD dissertation, Charles University in Prague, 2014) 88; Michal Ruzicka, "Unveiling What Should Remain Hidden: Ethics and Politics of Researching Marginal People," *Österreichische Zeitschrift für Soziologie* 41:2 (2016) 161.

6 Manuela Cantón Delgado, "Stigma and Ethno-Genesis amongst Pentecostal Gitanos in Spain," in Thurfjell and Marsh, *Romani Pentecostalism*, 75–88.

7 Marsh and Thurfjell, "Introduction," in Marsh and Thurfjell, *Romani Pentecostalism*, 13.

8 Elin Strand locates it in this historical moment, arguing that its growth "met a need for spiritual rehabilitation following the suffering and losses of 1939–1945." Elin Strand, "'One Scattered Race like Stars in the Sight of God': The International Gypsy Evangelical Church," in Thurfjell and Marsh, *Romani Pentecostalism*, 109–26. Régis Laurent refers to the Gypsies that were in Nazi concentration camps and were now in a country still inhospitable to them. Régis Laurent, "On the Genesis of Gypsy Pentecostalism in Brittany," in Thurfjell and Marsh, *Romani Pentecostalism*, 31–40.

9 Le Cossec, who is non-Roma, eventually became known as the "Apostle to the Gypsies." Laurent, "On the Genesis of Gypsy Pentecostalism in Brittany," 33, 39. René Zanellato is the current international coordinator and founder of mission work in Russia and central Asia.

10 Thomas A. Acton, "New Religious Movements among Roma, Gypsies and Travellers: Placing Romani Pentecostalism in an Historical and Social Context," in Thurfjell and Marsh, *Romani Pentecostalism*, 26. See also René Zanellato (GATIEF@ orange.fr), "G.A.T.I.E.F 2014 Worldwide Report, Life and Light Mission" (2014).

11 Magdalena Slavkova, "'Prestige' and Identity Construction amongst Pentecostal Gypsies in Bulgaria," in Thurfjell and Marsh, *Romani Pentecostalism*, 60; Sorin Gog, "Post-Socialist Religious Pluralism: How do Religious Conversions of Roma Fit into the Wider Landscape? From Global to Local Perspectives," in A. Boscoboinik and F. Ruegg, eds., *Transitions: Nouvelles identites rom en Europe centrale & orientale* (Brussels: Universite libre de Bruxelles, 2009) 93–108.

12 Manuela Cantón-Delgado, "Gypsy Leadership, Cohesion and Social Memory in the Evangelical Church of Philadelphia," *Social Compass* 64:1 (2017) 76–91.

13 For example, a Roma migrant church in Luton, England is made of the Rugul Aprins [Burning Bush] movement from Toflea, Romania. This is the place where a revival began in the 1990s and resulted in 80 to 90 percent of the village converting to Christianity. Roma Pentecostals from Lom, Bulgaria have four "daughter churches" in Germany. However, these examples are not particularly missional outside their own Roma group.

14 Veselin Popov and Elena Marushiakova, "The Relations of Ethnic and Confessional Consciousness of Gypsies in Bulgaria." *FACTA UNIVERSITATIS - Series Philosophy, Sociology, Appropriation and Social Psychology and History* 6 (1999) 81–89. Melody J. Wachsmuth, "Roma Christianity in Central and Eastern Europe: Challenges, Opportunities for Mission, Modes of Significance," in Corneliu Constantineanu, Marcel V. Măcelaru, Anne-Marie Kool and Mihai Himcinschi, eds., *Mission in Central and Eastern Europe: Realities, Perspectives, Trends* (Oxford: Regnum Books, 2017) 555–56. For example, a qualitative and mapping study commissioned by The Institute of Ethnology of the Slovak Academy of Sciences on Slovakia, see Tatiana Podolinska and Tomaš Hrustič, "Religion as a Path to Change? The Possibilities of Social Inclusion of the Roma in Slovakia" (Friedrich Ebert Stiftung, 2010). On Bulgaria: Miroslav Atanasov, "Gypsy Pentecostals: The Growth of the Pentecostal Movement among the Roma in Bulgaria and Its Revitalization of Their Communities" (a PhD dissertation, Asbury Theological Seminary, 2008).

15 Atanasov, "Gypsy Pentecostals," 273.

16 Ripka, *Pentecostalism in Slovakia*, 40.

17 Thurfjell and Marsh, "Introduction," in Thurfjell and Marsh, *Romani Pentecostalism*, 11. Agustina Carrizo-Reimann, "The Forgotten Children of Abraham: Iglesia Evangelica Misionera Biblica Rom of Buenos Aires," *Romani Studies* 21:2 (2011) 161–76.

18 Ripka, *Pentecostalism in Slovakia*, 80, 81.

19 Melody J. Wachsmuth, "Separated Peoples: The Roma as Prophetic Pilgrims in Eastern Europe," *International Bulletin of Missionary Research* 37:3 (2013) 145–50.

20 Acton, "New Religious Movements," 29.

21 Thurfjell and Marsh, "Introduction," in Thurfjell and Marsh, *Romani Pentecostalism*, 15.

22 Tatiana Podolinská, "Questioning the Theory of Deprivation: Pentecostal Roma in Slovakia," in Thurfjell and Marsh, *Romani Pentecostalism*, 89.

23 Cantón-Delgado, "Gypsy Leadership," 3.

24 Acton, "New Religious Movements," 23; Cantón-Delgado, "Gypsy Leadership," 9.

25 The author's interviews and conversations with individuals and church leaders from Romania, Serbia, and Croatia (2013–17). Also Cantón-Delgado, "Gypsy Leadership," 8.

26 Johannes Ries, "The Cultural Dynamics of Romani/Gypsy Ethnicity and Pentecostal Christianity," in Thurfjell and Marsh, *Romani Pentecostalism*, 127–40.

27 Thurfjell and Marsh, "Introduction," in Thurfjell and Marsh, *Romani Pentecostalism*, 11.

28 Action, "New Religious Movements," 30.

29 Interviews and conversations by author in Apatin, Serbia, March, 2017.

30 Murat Önsoy and Zeynep Arkan Tuncel, "The Case of the Western Balkan Roma: A Litmus Test for Normative Power Europe? *Hacettepe University Journal of Economics and Administrative Sciences* 35:1 (2017) 52.

31 Önsoy and Tuncel, "The Case of the Western Balkan Roma," 41–65.

32 Different bodies conduct these reports. For example, the *Roma Inclusion Index 2015*, Human Rights Watch, Council of Europe, and European Commission.

33 Önsoy and Tuncel, "The Case of the Western Balkan Roma," 57.

34 Several articles and accounts have been written about Leskovac, including an interview from Else Stanković: http://www.rollinghills.org/Websites/rollinghills/files/Content/2452995/SerbiaWEB-2012.pdf

Also, see Wachsmuth, "Roma Christianity," 559; Melody J. Wachsmuth, "Missional Reorientation—God's Mission as the Intersection of Surprise and Constancy," *Kairos: Evangelical Journal of Theology* 7:2 (Zagreb, Croatia, 2013) 209–20.

35 The responders include: Đeno and Biljana Nikolić, interview by author, Darda, Croatia, March 14, 2017; Aleksandar Subotin, interview by author, Kucura, Serbia, March 18, 2017; Erman Salković, interview by author, Zemun, Serbia, March 28, 2017; Miki Kamberović, Šerif Bakić, Rama Raimović, Vladica Idic, email reply to Interview Questions, March 24, 2017; Zvezdan Bakić, Interview by author, Aptain, Serbia, March 19, 2017; and Selim Alijević, email reply to Interview questions, April 5, 2017.

36 Interview with B. Nikolić.

37 Interview details are found in note 35.

38 In March 2017, I was in a Romanian-speaking Roma community of 5000 people. My cultural guide was a young woman who was twenty years old and attending a university in a large city. She was the only person from this community who had gone on to higher education, but some people disapproved of this. My hosts told me, "I think this is not good that she keeps going to school." Their priority value is on closeness of family. In this community, pursuing education past the eighth grade or to high school is viewed negatively, particularly as it takes her away from her family and postpones her own marriage and family.

39 Cantón-Delgado, "Gypsy Leadership," 12.

40 Strand, "One Scattered Race," 113, 114.

41 In the numerous interviews I have conducted, visions and dreams can play a key role in conversion, or as a message of comfort and love, a warning, a "redirect," or even condemnation. Church leaders in the past have discussed the necessity to "test these messages" to ensure that they are from God and align with the teaching of the Bible (Wachsmuth, "Separated Peoples").

42 Michal Ruzicka, "Unveiling What Should Remain Hidden: Ethics and Politics of Researching Marginal People," *Österreichische Zeitschrift für Soziologie* 41:2 (2016) 160.

43 For example, a person can have the appropriate level of education but have trouble obtaining a job when the employer sees he or she is Roma.

44 One pastor said that the relationship between Serbians and Roma was better because the Serbians in his area were now as poor as, or poorer than, the Roma, but the Roma had more survival skills in this particular economic climate. Another pastor said things were much improved.

45 Attitudes of prejudice can be difficult to quantify or qualify. For example, a young Roma woman, a trained hairdresser, told me that she cannot get a job because she is Roma. In truth, she has not tried. However, this ambiguity is set in the context of my own observations of the deep prejudice (through actions and comments from the majority) as well as listening to numerous Roma accounts of direct prejudice. On the other hand, occasionally someone tells an account of an open reception when prejudice is expected.

46 Using Gypsy with a lower case "g" indicates an insult.

47 Wachsmuth, "Roma Christianity," 565.

48 Laurent, "On the Genesis," 36, 37.

49 Stephen B. Bevans and Roger P. Schroeder, *Constants in Context: A Theology of Mission for Today* (Maryknoll, NY: Orbis, 2004) 399.

50 Zvezdan Bakić, Conversations with author, Apatin, Serbia, March, 2017.

51 Ruzicka, "Unveiling," 147–64.

52 Bevans and Schroeder, *Constants*, 393.

RESTORING LOVE TO THE INTELLECTUAL LIFE

R. R. RENO

Spiritus 2.1–2 (2017) 119–127
http://digitalshowcase.oru.edu/spiritus/

Editor's note. Reno gave this address to the faculty of Oral Roberts University on January 9, 2017. It appears here in its original form.

*M*idway through my career as a college professor, I began to have serious misgivings about contemporary academic culture. I don't mean worries about political correctness or the overwhelming bias toward left-wing politics, although these are discouraging. Instead, my concerns revolved around a superficial and false intellectualism encouraged by higher education today. Skepticism and irony are pervasive. Students and faculty are trained to avoid being duped by advertisers, ideologues, and other hucksters of snake oil wisdom, and this goal has become more important than affirming truth.

Our academic culture encourages this mentality. As I've put it in a number of essays I've written recently,[1] when professors get together to talk about the goals of higher education, they almost always unite around the notion of "critical thinking," which in practice means dis-enchanting students by raising doubts and giving priority to questions rather than answers.

In itself, critical thinking can be a good thing in the intellectual life. Both the Greek philosophical tradition and the Old Testament put strong emphases on critique. Socrates was famous for questioning of conventional wisdom. The prophets of Israel pronounce words of judg-ment against Israel's tendency to slide toward idolatry. In both cases, critical thinking purifies by exposing falsehoods *as* false. This is surely a necessary first step toward affirming truths *as* true. To develop as an intellectual, the dross of error needs to be burned away.

Today, however, critical thinking is put forward as the essence of the intellectual life, not an aid in its development. As a consequence, we lose sight of something more basic. An intellectual needs to *desire* truth, because it is something we presently lack and must go outside of ourselves to find. This means that the root of the intellectual life is love. To love something is to seek an ever-greater union with it, which is exactly what a genuine intellectual desires in relation to truth.

The term that Greek thinkers and early Christians used to describe the overall pursuit of truth and the full cultivation of the life of the mind was *philosophy*, the love of wisdom, not *sophiology*, the rational study of wisdom. They recognized—and, again, this was true of biblically-influenced Christian thinkers just as much as pagan Greek ones—that we will never gain a larger view of reality unless we aspire to it. Larger truths are elusive. We can't grasp them unless we're animated by love's sometimes reckless passion. And passion is exactly what today's emphasis on critical thinking tends to work against.

Moments of Insight

In the mid-1990s I taught a number of times in Lithuania. The country had only recently secured its independence from the Soviet Union. Communism was officially atheistic, which meant that nobody was permitted to study theology. A courageous and indomitable woman, Egle Laumenskaite, invited me to come to teach a short course on postmodernism and theology. After listening to my lecture on Jacques Derrida, a figure whom I regard as an important spiritual theorist of postmodern nihilism, she said to me, "Derrida is following in the tradition of ancient skepticism."

Her comment immediately struck me as correct. Derrida was a particularly talented proponent of "critical thinking." His distinctive method, called Deconstruction, has a technical meaning, but we can see it in fairly simple terms. Deconstruction seeks to weaken truth, just as skepticism in ancient philosophy sought to neutralize the power of truth claims. In both cases, moreover, the weakening is proposed as humanizing rather than nihilistic. Released from loves' desire for transcendent truth, ancient figures such as Sextus Empiricus promise that we can live more calmly and at peace. If nothing is worth fighting for, nobody will fight. If nothing is worth sacrificing for, nobody will be required to make painful sacrifices. Thus, Derrida's deconstruction and the ancient skeptical tradition do not counsel despair. They aim to make life more live-able by dissuading us from desiring truth.

The same can be said about Epicurus and Lucretius and the tradition of ancient materialism. I've come to see that materialism also functions as a disenchanting philosophy. If we recognize that everything is reducible to material processes, we can be released from anxieties about the meaning of life, allowing us to just get on with our lives. The idea here is not to depress us with meaninglessness. Instead, Epicurus thought that materialism brings freedom from despair precisely because it disabuses us of higher aspirations.

In the years since that remarkable experience in Lithuania, I have become more and more sensible of the moral allure of critical thinking. It rarely takes the elaborate form of Derridian deconstruction. Nor does it usually adopt a radical skepticism or thoroughgoing materialism. But critical thinking in its present forms always involves disenchantment. If a young person comes to college with strong religious beliefs, many educators think that he needs to be challenged by "critical thinking." The same goes for someone with traditional moral convictions, especially when they concern male-female relations, sex, marriage, and family. In an academic culture of "critical thinking," the problem here is not one of truth or falsehood. At issue is the *intensity* of conviction, which our society regards as dangerous. Critical thinking, therefore, isn't meant to be a corrective stage in a larger pursuit of truth. The goal is disenchantment for its own sake. Loyalties need to be weakened so that students will be more tolerant, more accepting, and more inclusive.

Sextus Empiricus and Epicurus did not have these social goals in mind. Their skeptical and materialist outlooks promised a gospel of sorts. It was felt to be a consolation to know that nothing matters. And if you think about it, that makes sense. Life is full of disappointments, and, of course, death casts its dark shadow. Under these circumstances, nihilism need not bring despair but instead offers peace of mind. Nothing matters—and so we can relax and need not worry too much over the meaning of our lives.

To some degree, the recession of Christianity's influence in the West contributes to the enthusiasm for "critical thinking" and disenchantment. If we must face our guilt and shame without the promise of God's forgiveness, it makes sense to explain away human freedom as an illusion, as many materialists do, or to argue for moral relativism, which is the skeptical solution. Both approaches weaken moral truth, which in turn weakens unpleasant feelings of guilt and shame.

The same goes for death. St. Paul mocked death—"O death, where is thy sting? O grave, where is thy victory?" (1 Cor 15:55). In doing so, he relied on the resurrection of Christ. Today's unbelievers do not so much mock death as downplay it with talk of the "circle of life," or encourage resignation, which is the most common approach.

To these trends favoring disenchantment I would like to add our increasing feelings of political and social impotence. The democratic projects of modernity seem to be coming to an end, replaced now by a technocratic regime of expertise. In these circumstances, ironic detachment functions as a consolation, a way to manage our suspicion that our lives don't matter all that much in an increasingly globalized system.

In sum: critical thinking has emerged as the highest ambition of higher education because it weakens convictions. This weakening is sought for its own sake and not as a means to the greater end of guiding students toward a firmer and stronger devotion to truth. Today, we prize disenchantment as a therapy of the soul. Our goal in higher education is to encourage the development of accepting, non-judgmental personalities rather than cultivating a potentially fierce and jealous love of truth.

Two Objections

When I speak on this topic, people often point out that a great deal of higher education engages in a positive pedagogy that confidently inculcates into students strong convictions about truth. The natural sciences provide an obvious example, as do technical disciplines in the STEM fields. This objection accurately portrays what goes on in classes in electrical engineering, nursing, and physics. But it does not contradict my main point. From Pascal I learned an important truth about the life of the mind, which is that science provides us with firm but existentially inconsequential truths. The STEM fields are not oriented toward truths that illuminate the meaning of life. They do not help us understand how we should live nor what we should life for. As a consequence, the postmodern imperative of disenchantment need not bother itself with the first and second laws of thermodynamics. We can have a scientific and technological culture that is thoroughly disenchanted. In fact, a sure strategy for promoting disenchantment is to insist that the only "real" truths are scientific ones, for that weakens truth, not by encouraging relativism, but instead by encouraging scientism.

The second objection comes when some point out that today's educational environment is characterized by a sometimes fierce political correctness that's enforced with a great deal of zeal. This suggests, critics say, a selective application of critical thinking rather than wholesale disenchantment. I find this objection unpersuasive as well.

Political correctness is best understood as enforced disenchantment rather than a rival system of strong convictions. Take a look at the terms of abuse. The transgressors of political correctness are not criticized for being *wrong*. They are described as "judgmental" or "bigoted." The sin is not against truth; it's against tolerance or inclusion or diversity, depending on the circumstances. The paradox of the contemporary university culture that celebrates critical thinking and, at the same time, enforces an elaborate code of conduct is apparent, not real. What we have today is a moralistic anti-moralism, one that denounces strong beliefs as "divisive" and "hateful," while announcing itself committed to affirmation and acceptance. The object in both the politically correct judgmentalism *and* a disenchanted non-judgmentalism is the same. What we want today is the weakening of strong truths, not for the sake of truth, but in order to make the world a better place.

Enchantment

We need to be challenged, and our society begs for reformation. But it is important to recognize that the solution to our captivity to error and indifference to injustice is a pedagogy of enchantment that enflames us with a love of and devotion to truth, not the way of disenchantment, which seeks to cultivate indifference.

As a young teacher I was knocked out of a complacent commitment to "critical thinking" when I taught St. Augustine's *Confessions*. After reading a book of ancient philosophy, Augustine embarks on an intellectual journey. After reading other philosophers, he comes to believe that God is the all-good creator. Then he attends church and listens to fine sermons. He becomes convinced of the truth of Christianity. In a certain sense he believes, yet he cannot free himself from his loyalty to falsehood. He twists and turns but cannot break the chains that bind him. It's too bloodless, therefore, to speak of false beliefs, as if we can just check our math, as it were, and cure ourselves of error. Any consequential belief is best understood as a love, which means false beliefs are false loves. For that reason, even though Augustine saw the error of his beliefs, he could not be free from their falsehood. Only a true love can overcome the power of a false love. We need to be romanced away from error, which is exactly how Augustine describes his conversion and that of his friend, Alypius. Addressing God, he says, "You have pierced our hearts with the arrow of your love."

A similar view can be found in Plato's *Symposium*, where Socrates recounts his own teacher's account of love's power to propel us toward the highest truths. But I prefer the vivid imagery of the opening, allegorical chapters of the Book of Proverbs (1—9). There, the men of the city allow themselves to be seduced by prostitutes and loose women. This sexualized image is commonly used in the Old Testament to connote the worship of false idols. In the Book of Proverbs, Lady Wisdom tries to teach the men of the city the error of their ways by recounting the bad consequences that will follow from their false loves. One could say that Lady Wisdom deploys critical thinking in order to disenchant the bewitching idols. Such an approach, however, does not work. So Lady Wisdom changes her pedagogical strategy. She retreats to her palace, lays out fine food and wine, and then sends her most beautiful maidservants out into the city to call the men to her banquet (9:1–6). "Come," beckons Lady Wisdom, "eat of my bread and drink the wine I have mixed." She seeks to counter the seductions of error by presenting truth in an even more alluring form. She enchants, and her enchantment leads the men of the city out of their love of what is false and toward a love of truth.

If we wish to cultivate a desire for wisdom, we need to give priority to enchantment rather than disenchantment in higher education. That need not mean discarding critical thinking. As I said earlier, pressing hard questions is part of the intellectual tradition in the West, as we see in Socrates and the Old Testament prophets. But critical questioning needs to take place within a more encompassing pedagogy of love and devotion.

Tradition plays a key role in this kind of pedagogy. *Traditio* means handing or passing on, the transmission of a precious inheritance. Higher education has been characterized by rituals such as matriculation and graduation, because students are being initiated into something sacred. Giving priority to functionalism and efficiency tends to downplay these rituals. Another enemy of ritual is an anxiety about hierarchy and desire to make everyone feel equal. These are among the many ways in which we disenchant all our social relations, and they need to be resisted. Ritual incubates devotion, and if we're to escape the gravitational pull of disenchantment we should encourage the re-ritualization of academic life. Perhaps professors should wear their academic gowns on a regular basis!

The very name "professor" suggests a form of life that provides role models of devotion. A PhD does not train one to teach. Instead, it is training *in* a discipline. At its best, this kind of graduate study, which takes place over many years, forms a person in a deep way, making him devoted to the distinctive methods and achievements of his discipline. For this reason, a teacher in higher education does not teach in the same way a primary or secondary teacher approaches instruction. He wants his students to learn, of course. But over the course of a semester, a genuine college-level class in philosophy, psychology, or physics needs to enact or in some way "perform" the discipline. So-called student-centered learning is a mistaken concept. A pedagogy of enchantment is professor-centered, not in a selfish sense, but because student are invited into that which the professor professes.

Taken as a whole, however, higher education needs to be more than a menu of diverse disciplines from which students chose. There needs to be a core or canon that serves as a common, shared focus for the academic community. We invariably argue about what that core or canon should be. A pedagogy of enchantment is not static and authoritarian. However, we need to make a promise to students: If you devote yourselves to *these* key books and *this* tradition, you will not just become more learned, you will see the world in a fuller, more comprehensive way. If you study Plato, Aristotle, Augustine, Aquinas, Calvin, and the other great figures in our tradition, you will attain a margin of wisdom. At a place like ORU, the Bible should have pride of place, of course. In an important way, a core or canon outlines a path of ascent, which we need if higher education is to merit its claim to go higher.

There are other features of an educational culture that enchant. Good lectures are performances that, at the best, draw us in. A well-run seminar gathers students into a shared spirit of inquiry. Book-laden shelves in faculty offices remind us that our love of learning has no end. But I cannot outline all the details. Every institution is unique, and in any event what is crucial is the teleology of an educational culture—the end, goal, or ambition of pedagogy—not its administrative structure or range of subjects. As you certainly know, the Bible itself can be taught in ways that disenchant young people who harbor hopes that they might find lasting truths in that sacred text—or it can be taught in ways that encourage those hopes.

Our Difficult Moment

We live in an era of weakening. A consensus now dominates that regards strong, life-engaging truths as a threat. We've even reached a point at which the plain truth of our bodies—that we are male or female—is being called into question. To speak of "gender assigned at birth" is to engage in a radical disenchantment.

I don't want to engage in a tiresome refutation of transgender ideology, which is in any event beside the point. This ideology is part of a moral and spiritual project, not an intellectual one. It seeks a therapy of the soul oriented toward a general indifference toward truth and open-ended acceptance of others. This sort of approach is seen as necessary in order to usher in a utopia of equal freedom, which means the universal affirmation of everyone in whatever way they wish to be affirmed.

Instead, I want to draw attention to our situation as educators, which is difficult. If today's secular culture discourages young people from thinking that our bodies can speak to us with clarity about the truth of who we are, then it will difficult to encourage students to seek the moral and spiritual truths that are more remote and uncertain than our male and female bodies.

In our present circumstances, therefore, the last thing we need is facile talk of "critical thinking." A contemporary reading of Shakespeare may teach useful lessons about race, class, gender, and other human realities that we must reckon with. But the direction is downward. Critical analysis, as its presently understood, is reductionist in the sense that it tends to dissolve complex human realities into lower things such as instinct, self-interest, and the will-to-power. This downward move disenchants, and truth's spiritual possibilities are limited.

God calls us toward him. The church fathers spoke of fallen man as bent over, looking downward. The Holy Spirit unbends the human spirit, raising our eyes upward. We need to recover the upward movement in higher education. It won't come by appeals to authority, nor will it be made possible by pious exhortations. Instead, we need a pedagogy of enchantment, one that is willing to entertain metaphysical ambition, and one that takes the risk of fanning in young people the always-present yet presently dampened desire for the transcendent.

R. R. Reno is editor of *First Things,* America's premier journal of religion and public life.

Note

1 *Fighting the Noonday Devil — and Other Essays Personal and Theological* (Grand Rapids, MI: Wm. B. Eerdmans, 2011).

RESTORING TRUTH TO THE INTELLECTUAL LIFE
A RESPONSE TO RUSTY RENO

WILLIAM EPPERSON

Spiritus 2.1–2 (2017) 129–136
http://digitalshowcase.oru.edu/spiritus/

Editor's note. ORU English professor William Epperson drafted the first version of this response after reading two essays by Reno that faculty were asked to read before Reno addressed them. Encouraged by the response of several peers and the request of *Spiritus,* he revised his response, which *Spiritus* is pleased to publish.

*R*usty Reno, in his address "Restoring Love to the Intellectual Life," delivered to the Oral Roberts University faculty on January 9, 2017, centered his remarks on the over-emphasis of critical thinking in modern academia—an emphasis that "in practice means disenchanting students by raising doubts and giving priority to questions rather than answers." Reno finds the pedagogical aim has become training students and faculty "to avoid being duped by advertisers, ideologues, and other hucksters of snake oil wisdom, and this goal has become more important than affirming truth."

But is not critical thinking more acutely needed now than ever? With the flood of information, much of it false or biased, passed on to society by public media—television and radio, but perhaps more so by irresponsible internet postings on social media such as Twitter and Facebook—teachers must not only equip students with knowledge of the old-fashioned logical fallacies, but also encourage fact-checking sources like Snopes.com to establish the validity and credibility of what they hear and see on the informational outlets so available to them. Indeed, Reno affirms that "critical thinking purifies by exposing false-hoods *as* false . . . a necessary first step toward affirming truths *as* true." Perhaps the legitimate need to teach critical thinking that we find so urgent now reveals a more pervasive weakness in our society's intellectual health. We are experiencing the decay of belief in what have been called the "Transcendentals"—objective truth, yes, but also objective goodness and beauty—values that were the foundation of education from the Classical age to the Modern period. They were what our education aimed for; we shaped learning to lead students to see, acknowledge, and love the Good, the True, and the Beautiful. These values were our standards by which we structured our culture, measured our laws and customs, evaluated our arts, and organized our institutions. Even while we acknowledged that we had no perfect vision of these qualities, that we are always growing toward apprehending them more clearly, they remained our measuring rods that we used to make and revise laws to better reflect justice, to encourage our arts to better delight and instruct us, to guide our science and technologies toward humane applications.

Today we are living off the shrinking capital of these "Transcendentals." Even our word "values" has eroded. "Values" are cut to tastes and feeling, individualized and not subject to judgment. The "values" of many today are described by the early Hemingway protagonist of *The Sun Also Rises*, Jake Barnes, who defines immorality as "things that made you disgusted afterward." Jake had reason for his disillusionment, having been wounded in a war he could not understand or justify. Young people today, finding no clear truth or goodness to guide them, repeat this individualized moral perspective under their *unum necessarium*, the one virtue they put over all others, tolerance. Of course, a degree of tolerance, we all agree, is a good thing, but it is absolutely demanded, in unqualified form, if we are all living according to our own standards, our own tastes, our own "goodness." In such a subjective world, where no absolute goodness is acknowledged, no one has the right to correct anyone else, for there is no objective moral measuring rod.

The modern secular university, as Reno warns, does discourage belief in objective truth, goodness, or beauty. An example comes to mind: in the 1980's a noble experiment at the University of Kansas was brought to an end. The Pearson College Integrated Humanities Program, formed by three highly honored graduate professors, John Senior, Dennis Quinn, and Franklyn Nelick, led undergraduate students through the classic works that formed Western civilization, from Homer, Plato, Aristotle, Aeschylus and Sophocles, through St. Augustine and St. Thomas, to modern philosophers and writers. Exposed to these thinkers who expressed the "Perennial Philosophy" of an objective truth, goodness, and beauty, students reacted as if they had found water for a deep thirst they had not even known they had. They fell in love with these old, old truths that had been cast aside by today's intellectual culture, some even converting to Catholic Christianity. The University reacted by taking away the previous policy of awarding General Education humanities credit for the twelve hours taught in the Integrated Humanities Program. The publicly stated reason? The three professors all believed in an objective Truth that should be an aim of study, rather than a relative truth that university faculty need to be presenting to students. According to University officials, students must be encouraged to question their previous ideas about truth so they can freely determine their own truth; professors must model the diversity of truth, and students must be taught to participate in their own construction of truth.

Reno's diagnosis of the major problem of American education is right on target, I believe, as it relates to public education, particularly higher education. It is less relevant to the work and orientation of Christian colleges that have a cadre of teachers who still believe in the traditional "Transcendentals" of goodness, truth, and beauty. The realities of our universe, we believe, reveal these qualities for they, the qualities and the creatures, originate in their source, the creator God; humans, as creatures who most clearly bear the image of God, find these qualities within themselves, attenuated by sin and the resulting weakness of the will, but still inherent in our souls. We work to help students see and love these in the world around them, in their fellow humans, and in the works of humans—in the arts and sciences and institutions in which they participate.

Our students need to learn to be more critical thinkers, to promote their clear thinking and to avoid logical fallacies—but not to the point of a skeptical distrust of everything their attention falls on. Unfortunately, the contemporary social and cultural environment does, in fact, encourage such radical skepticism. For many creative people, the center no longer holds; there is no ordering principle giving coherence and meaning to reality. Beauty is no longer the central aim of the arts, nor is goodness or truth. These qualities that guided traditional arts have little or no power today; they have been rendered impotent by a pervading atmosphere of subjectivity and relativity. Sensation and shock are the effects desired by some well-known artists—musicians, painters, even writers—whose material (words) would seem to tie them inseparably to meaning. Rock musicians have shocked audiences since Peter Townshend of *The Who* shattered his guitar on stage in 1968. Guitar shattering has marked concert climaxes since—with Eddy van Halen, *Nirvana's* Kurt Cobain, *The Clash's* Paul Simonson, and even Jimi Hendrix destroying their instruments on stage, and to what end? Asked about this in a *Rolling Stone* interview in 1968, Peter Townshend said, "it's an act, it's an instant, and it really is meaningless." Yes, it is meaningless, but it is not without sensation, without shock. The musicians that followed Townshend's "act," his "instant," simply tried to replicate his shock—with diminishing effect as the years passed; yesterday's shock is, as they say, so "yesterday."

Contemporary painters and other artists also substitute shock for Truth or Beauty. British artist Chris Ofili attempts "to jolt viewers into an expanded frame of reference" by daubing his portrait titled "The Holy Virgin Mary" with elephant dung. Andres Serrano imposes shock on his viewers with a photograph of a crucifix immersed in a jar of urine (his own, he informs us). And experimental writers, mainly writing in the 1970's, produce incomprehensible poems and "stories." But since shock is an effect impossible to sustain, the lasting power of such displays of sensationalism is quite evanescent; one can only be appalled at the destruction of guitars a couple of times, after that the shock becomes a cliché. Performance art—fortunately, brief and impermanent, but drawing crowds of voyeuristic viewers—may be the perfect art for many in today's audiences, who value sensation and originality, but are incapable of attention, reflection, or meditation—and skeptical of any hint of meaning.

I know these are extreme examples, but what kind of society permits—indeed, encourages—even a modicum of interest in such things? Students can hardly be blamed for doubting the significance of the arts, just as they doubt the credibility of politics, the value and dependability of a free press, and the integrity of corporations. Ultimately, they doubt the validity of their own ethics. They learn from contemporary philosophy and literary theory that truth, goodness, and beauty are all relative—merely cultural constructs that they, as "educated" elite, must relinquish. What impels them to forsake their trust in the old values? Perhaps they have a belief in human progress that is shaped on the evident progress in scientific knowledge and technological advancement. Perhaps they are seeking a more esoteric spiritual enlightenment. Perhaps they are enamored of some principle or idea that they trust will save the world. Or perhaps they simply are bored with the old verities, finding revolutionary notions and actions to be more interesting.

C. S. Lewis asserted "two propositions" in "The Poison of Subjectivism," an essay initially published in *Religion and Life* in 1943 and often republished:

1. The human mind has no more power of inventing a new value than of planting a new sun in the sky or a new primary colour in the spectrum.

2. Every attempt to do so consists in arbitrarily selecting some maxim of traditional morality, isolating it from the rest, and erecting it into an *unum necessarium*.

Beyond today's students being taught the subjectivity of all values, they are learning that gender and race are also merely cultural constructs, having no basis for a claim of objectivity. Even their sense of themselves as a "self" is not immune to these deconstructive tendencies. Traditional man knew and trusted "reality," knowing without question that what "is" cannot simultaneously be "not is." They trusted that an idea cannot be both true and false, light cannot be the absence of light, goodness cannot be evil. Traditional man knew "I am, therefore I think," before Descartes, anticipating the new philosophy of subjectivism, threw us into the modern world by his maxim, "I think, therefore I am." Of course, students don't receive these ideas directly; few of them read the philosophers, probably fewer read the literary theorists—the feminists, the gender critics, the racial critics, the Marxist critics, or the whole slew of other voices—but they pick these notions up as they filter down into commonplace daily life and assumptions. They too often accept the attitude of "if it works for you, that's great." Their religion is what feels good to them; their worship is what pleases their senses; their morality is too often of the "early Hemingway" type—avoiding what makes you feel "disgusted afterward."

If their thinking is confused by subjectivity, their hold on the real is similarly imperiled by an education biased toward abstraction; we teach them to prioritize the intellectual habits of analyzing—categorizing, dealing with principles and universals, demanding the higher skills of intellect before the foundation of *experience* has instructed their hearts to *love* the real. What if we, like the ancient Greeks, emphasized the body and the senses first? What if we taught the joy of music, with its order, harmonies, melodies, proportions—not as concepts, but as sense experiences, as something beautiful and joyful—prior to teaching math, where these same qualities exist as intellectual *aesthetic* experiences? What if we told stories as the Greeks did, for the sake of the stories, and thereby shaped children's hearts to love the brave, the good, the hopeful, the true—by their identifying with the stories' protagonists rather than by didactic moralizing? They might then have characters that were good soil for the growth of morals, ethics, right reason, and profound religious sensibilities.

One of the most profound treatments of the grace of forgiveness is Shakespeare's *The Tempest*, in which Prospero forgives his enemies—including his traitorous brother—and frees the servant/spirit Ariel. As the epilogue of the play, Prospero seeks freedom for the players, invoking the applause of the audience. This is the clear theme of the play—a testament to the power of forgiveness and freedom. But today, students reading the play are told by post-colonial critics that the play is really about European exploitation of native peoples. Prospero is no longer a Christ figure extending forgiveness and freedom, but a villain—at best, a powerful man who is simply ignorant of his greedy exploitive motives. Caliban is no longer a brutish savage in need of redemption, but the victim of colonial power. Never mind that he too was not native to the island (his mother, the witch Sycorax, had been banished to the uninhabited island because of her crimes); never mind that Caliban turns from his perversion of Prospero's teaching him language—which he uses to curse—and repents and resolves to "sue for grace" when Prospero acknowledges him at the play's ending. In this way, the contemporary theory replaces the earlier affirmation of the reality of sin (betrayal and idolatry) and the greater power of forgiveness. The abstract theory distorts the literal action and meaning of the play. Today's readers may plead, "But we do not believe in forgiveness as a spiritual power; it may have psychological benefits, of course." The people of the late 16th century did believe in it, Shakespeare and his audience believed in it, and when we moderns read earlier literature it would be to our advantage if we first try to see the world as they saw it, rather than rushing to impose our attitudes on the texts. Read the play as closely as possible as it was read or viewed contemporaneously, then we can discuss the differences between modern values and earlier values.

Fundamentally, I believe we need to reintroduce students to what is *real*, the natural world presented to our senses. From this base, that which is good, true, and beautiful can be imagined and affirmed. In my childhood, I had the freedom to explore the woods and ponds and rivers around my small town. I was not afraid to explore, to spend a day walking alone in the country, staring at plants, and flowers, rocks, and beetles. These drew me out of myself into experiences of loving relationship with natural things of beauty. I felt wonder as I watched a shower of "falling stars." I felt heavenly beauty as I saw a morning sunrise light up a golden river bluff and its green crowning hill. Such experiences led me to a hunger for the beauty of God, and for the echoes of that beauty reflected from earthly creatures, then from the beams of reflected beauty—and goodness and truth—of human arts.

I wonder about children today. They live according to their schedules, their soccer matches, their dance lessons. They have limited attention spans, their cell phones moving along from image to image quite briskly. A free 20 minutes is enough for ennui to set in; their most favored word is "boring." I hope I am simply exaggerating. Grandfathers have been seeing their beloved grandchildren—and their friends—going to the dogs since Aristotle. But when my 18-year-old students cannot enjoy a poem or have any idea what it is saying or any interest, I worry. They complain that the poem is too "abstract," when actually it is too concrete, its images too specific, individual, sharp, invoking real senses. A good poem demands they imagine it with their senses alive, that they connect its images into coherent patterns; in short, that they transform its concreteness and lack of abstraction into a more abstract meaning. And that action they feel incapable of doing. Distracted beyond any previous generation, they are not friends with natural reality, not used to "making meaning." Perhaps the first college class they should take as part of the "General Education" sequence should be "Backpacking"—with at least two strenuous trips into the backwoods and a couple of star-watching evenings required.

Two years ago, as I walked out of the Oral Roberts University Graduate Center building, making my way to my car, I happened to glance up into the sky to find, to my wonder, a skyscape unlike any I'd seen before. I stopped and simply stared—the whole sky was textured by parallel lines of cirrus clouds, arranged like squadrons of mounted troops across the heavens. I gazed in wonder at the beauty. Then students began to come out the GC doors, two or three girls immediately checking their phones, chatting, never looking up, never looking around, caught up in their own individual electronic worlds. Had they looked up at the amazing scene in the sky, they might have reflected briefly, they may have thought about this beauty, recovered it from their memories. They may have tried to write a poem.

We pay lip service to the Psalmist's affirmation, "the heavens declare the glory of God, and the firmament shows His handiwork." But do we care? Are we interested enough to look up?

William Epperson is a long-serving Professor of English at Oral Roberts University who is loved by many for his courage to speak candidly and his skill at speaking aptly.

REVIEWS

Messenger: Sydney Elton and the Making of Pentecostalism in Nigeria. By Ayodeji Abodunde. Lagos: Pierce Watershed, 2016. 479 pp.

*N*igeria has the largest constituency of Pentecostals and charismatics in Africa, representing three out of every ten Nigerians. While Israel O. Olofinjana (2011), Jesse Zink (2012), Nimi Wariboko (2014), Richard Burgess (2015) and Musa A. B. Gaiya (2015) have addressed this phenomenon, there has been little research about Sydney Granville Elton (1907–1987), one of the longest-serving Christian missionaries in Nigeria (1937–1987). In *Messenger: Sydney Elton and the Making of Pentecostalism in Nigeria*, historian Ayodeji Abodunde uses extensive primary sources, oral interviews, and analysis of secondary sources to explore the contributions of this key leader. It clearly demonstrates how Elton helped shape Pentecostalism in Nigeria through encouraging strong foundations; Pentecostal revival; ecumenical unity; charismatic renewal; and theological teaching.

Strong Foundations

The first three chapters cover the origins of the Apostolic Church in Nigeria and Elton's early involvement. The movement can be traced back to the 1917 founding of the Diamond Society, Lagos by David Ogunleye Odubanjo. Members embraced rigorous holiness teaching and rejected modern medicine. After 1923, the renamed Faith Tabernacle Church continued to spread as the Faith Tabernacle movement. During 1930, a great healing revival broke out through the ministry of Joseph Ayo Babalola, bringing thousands suddenly into the churches. In an attempt to allay violent harassment by the colonial authorities, a partnership was formed with the Apostolic Church in Great Britain.

In 1936, Sydney Elton, originally from Wolverhampton, England, was sent out by the Shrewsbury Apostolic Church to Ilesa area in western Nigeria. The following year, his wife Hannah and three-year-old daughter Grace, also joined him. Working closely with Apostolic Church leader, J. A. Babatope, Elton led church planting drives and trained up new leaders. However, tensions arose when Pentecostal missionaries began to question Babalola's interpretation of divine healing and complete rejection of medicine as idolatry. In 1940, the movement split and Babalola formed Nigerian Apostolic Church, while Babatope stayed loyal to Elton and the Apostolic Church.

Pentecostal Revival

Chapters Four to Six examine Elton's involvement in Pentecostal revivalism. After the 1940 split, the number of Apostolic Churches in the Ilesa Area decreased from almost 200 to only four assemblies. From Elton's base at Oke Oye, he helped build this back up to 125 churches. Babatope established Ilesa Bible School to train workers and Elton later took on the principalship. In 1945, Elton also became pioneer principal of a government-approved teacher training centre called Elementary Training Centre in Ilesa.

During 1951, the Canadian-originated Latter Rain movement reached Nigeria. Elton (107) writes that, "God broke us" in repentance from "dead works." Consequently, he spoke to crowds of up to 50,000 people and planted 150 churches. However, within a couple of years, the anti-Latter Rain faction of the Apostolic Church International Missionary Council in Bradford had condemned the revival. So, in 1954, Elton resigned and was apparently wiped from the records, as he does not even rate a mention in the extensive Apostolic Church history by T. N. Turnbull (1959).

Ecumenical Unity

The next three chapters explore Elton's focus on ecumenism in Nigeria and Ghana through his World Christian Crusade. Through this organisation, he hosted renowned preachers, such as David du Plessis, Gordon Lindsay and T. L. Osborn. As the only Pentecostal on the Christian Council of Nigeria, Elton also toured the United States of America and Great Britain. He founded the Nigeria Christian Fellowship as a network of independent churches and thousands of leaders were trained through his Bible school programs and correspondence courses. Ayodeji Abodunde (150) argues that this represented "the largest individual effort toward laying the foundation of Pentecostal doctrine in eastern Nigeria outside denominational boundaries."

During Nigeria's civil war (1967–1970), Elton founded Soul-winners Unlimited Nigeria which ran short-term schools of evangelism. By 1977, around 50,000 young people had been trained. To counter Communist literature, Elton's *Our Freedom* magazine circulated over 80,000 copies a month and his *Nigerian Herald of the Last Days* became his flagship publication. Elton also contributed articles to the popular *Pentecost* and distributed the international *Herald of His Coming*. Thus, Elton helped bring Nigeria into the global Pentecostal limelight.

Charismatic Renewal

Chapters Ten to Thirteen discuss Elton's role on tertiary campuses. He supported charismatic leaders, such as Tunde Joda, David Oyedepo, Bayo Famonure, Francis Wale Oke, Emiko Amotsuka, J. M. J. Emesim, Chukwuedozie Mba, Paul Nwachukwu, Augustine Nwodika and Emeka Eze. In 1975, Elton also helped found Calvary Productions which became the largest indigenous missionary organisation in Africa. Therefore, he is known as the 'father' of the charismatic renewal in Nigeria.

Another prominent leader mentored by Elton was Benson Andrew Idahosa who founded Christ for the Nations International Evangelistic Association which had over 700 churches. However, after Idahosa was ordained in Benin City as bishop (and later Archbishop) of the Church of God Mission, Elton became concerned about the negative influence of American Pentecostal materialism. Elton's condemnation of the prosperity gospel ultimately saw him ostracised from Nigerian Pentecostalism.

Theological Teaching

The final four chapters provide an analysis of Elton's theology which viewed the church as the prophetic voice of the nation. With the post-civil war rise of Communism, Elton increasingly described Jesus Christ as a radical revolutionary and he actively supported the Christian Students' Social

Movement and Christian Action Committee to foster Christian political engagement. He believed the church was to be a vehicle for cultural, political, economic, religious and social transformation.

Elton also called for a restoration of the five-fold ministry gifts and believed that denominationalism stifled revivalism. After 53 years of marriage, Hannah passed away. In 1984, Elton married Grace Delbridge but he died just three years later. His daughter, Ruth ultimately spent almost five decades serving in Nigeria. Ayodeiji Abodunde concludes that the Eltons contributed about 160 years to Nigeria – perhaps more than any other missionary family in the nation's history.

The primary contribution of this volume is that it provides a detailed biography of one of the most influential figures of Pentecostalism in Nigeria. Lapses in chronological order are occasionally distracting and further research needs to explore the missionary work of Hannah and Ruth Elton. Nevertheless, the author provides solid evidence for his case that Sydney Elton made a major contribution to Pentecostalism in Nigeria. As such, it is a thoroughly commendable work.

Denise A. Austin is Director of Accreditation and Standards and Associate Professor of History at Alphacrucis College (Australia), where she researches Australian Pentecostal history and the contribution of women to Pentecostalism.

The Spirit of Jesus Unleashed on the Church: Acts of the Early Christians in a Changing Culture. By Ron Clark. Eugene, OR: Cascade Books, 2016. 204 pp.

*R*on Clark is a pioneer pastor of a "missional" church (my term for a church which is very outward-looking and involved with the local community) in Portland, Oregon. His journey into and with this church plant gives him a specific and interesting perspective on the Book of Acts. This book offers brief commentary on Acts but seeks primarily to apply the message of Acts to the current situation in light of Clark's missional church experiences. Clark supplements this application with insights into Acts from his own studies and reading. The two perspectives come together awkwardly at times, but when they do interact successfully, profound insights result. Clark does not appear to be Pentecostal, but he believes strongly the Holy Spirit works in and through today's church powerfully, if the church is willing to adventure radically with Jesus.

This book is the third in a series: the first two were about the Old Testament prophets and the Gospel of Luke, and the volume on Luke is referred to frequently in this book. But both earlier books provide the basis for the introductory chapter, "How Did We Get Here?," which opens with a story of the author's conversations late one day with two unusual people in a light-rail train, one with hygiene issues and the other a marijuana user. His point is the need to engage with people where they are as the Spirit leads us. Perhaps if this were a Pentecostal book, it would have ended more dramatically, but Clark shows his willingness simply to engage with these people and not try to convert them. He then develops the Old Testament prophetic background about Israel's waiting for God's deliverance and the coming of Christ, leading to the coming of the Spirit to empower the first believers in Jesus as his witnesses. The conclusion is that the waiting time is over: now "Christians are not called to wait, they are called to go" (14), especially to the marginalized and outcasts of society. Clark shares his own story of being called to plant a church like this at the end of Chapter 1.

The rest of the book covers Acts largely in chronological order, arranged under three sections:

Should We Stay or Should We Go? (based on Acts 1—12)

An Empire Sent by the Spirit (based on Acts 13—20)

Enduring Resistance for the Sake of the Empire (based on Acts 21—28).

Several distinctive features of the book's discussion of Acts are worth noting. It emphasizes Acts as narrative and compares, for example, its account of Paul's life with that of Homer's heroes, although without implying that Acts is fictional. The work interacts intermittently with critical voices, for example, with Patricia Walters' contentions about the authorship of Acts (22). It also gives periodic insights from social scientific and other scholarship on Acts, for example, the intriguing suggestions about Paul's relationship with Sergius Paulus, the proconsul in Cyprus, which may even explain his adoption of the name Paul (93–94). Finally, the work uses the language of empire and resistance to disclose the theological emphasis of Acts, drawing on the canonical prophetic literature and its theme of restoration. This approach gives the reader both a historically contextual insight (contrasting with the Roman empire) and a fresh view of the Spirit's ongoing outreach in Acts. As a result, the author, for example, sees Acts not so much as an unfinished story (a common view) but as a finished story that climaxes with Paul's arrival in Rome, where he may speak about Jesus to all who visit his rented apartment. This action truly ends Acts: finally "there [is] no resistance" from the Jews and others to the gospel, "the gospel end[s] not at the seat of Judaism but that of the Gentile world" (for those formerly on the religious margins), and "the gospel end[s] with hospitality" as Paul welcomes seekers in Rome, even though he is a prisoner (171–172).

Sometimes the author's anecdotes do not relate well to the discussion of Acts; however, Clark's insights challenge and provoke thought. On the whole, then, this work approaches Acts as a book and its message for contemporary western churches in a refreshing way.

Jon K. Newton (PhD, Deakin University) is the Dean of Postgraduate Studies and Research at Harvest Bible College, Australia, and editor of the *Journal of Contemporary Ministry.*

Strangers to Fire: When Tradition Trumps Scripture. By Robert Graves, ed. Tulsa, OK: Empowered Life Academic, 2014. xxxvii + 561 pp.

*F*or the last three decades, the Rev. John F. MacArthur, Jr., popular evangelical author and radio Bible teacher, has raged against the Pentecostal-Charismatic Movement (PCM). Beginning in 1978, with his book, *The Charismatics,* again in 1993, with *Charismatic Chaos,* and most recently, in 2013, in the pages of *Strange Fire,* MacArthur attacks the PCM. While his earlier books sought to point out the theological weaknesses of the PCM, in *Strange Fire: The Danger of Offending the Holy Spirit with Counterfeit Worship*, he makes a full attack on not only the theological tenets of the PCM, but also upon the very essence of the PCM and labels it a "demonic delusion". MacArthur's central argument against the PCM is that of cessationism, i.e., that the *charismata,* or spiritual gifts and miracles, mentioned in the New Testament, have ceased to operate in the church, especially since the canon of the New Testament was finalized and such charismata are therefore no longer needed to authenticate the apostolic proclamation of the gospel. As a result, all claims about the contemporary occurrence of miraculous gifts are false and the occurrences themselves are counterfeits, at best, or demonic.

Several texts have answered MacArthur's attacks but none as ably as *Strangers to Fire: When Tradition Trumps Scripture*. This volume, edited by Robert W. Graves, director of the Foundation for Pentecostal Scholarship, addresses every aspect of MacArthur's challenges. Its thirty essays draw from classical Pentecostal and denominational and independent charismatic authors and address exegetical, theological, and historical questions raised by MacArthur. Several of the essays are reprinted from other publications, such as *Paraclete* and *Pneuma,* and five of the chapters are published posthumously (Essays by Andrew T. Floris, d. 2012; Melvin Hodges, d. 1988; Omer J. Sharp, d. 2006; Horace S. Ward, d. 2014 and David A. Womack, d. 2009.)

The list of contributors shows the breadth and depth of the scholarship of the work. A fair and balanced foreword by J. Lee Grady, former editor of *Charisma* magazine, honestly acknowledges that the PCM has its "fringe element" and "that MacArthur doesn't have to look hard to find examples of troublesome doctrines and quirky practices" (xxiv), but it also challenges MacArthur's blanket condemnation of all who believe "that God can speak to people today," including even Southern Baptist author Henry Blackaby, who certainly would not describe himself as Pentecostal or charismatic (xxiii).

The first section of *Stranger to Fire,* seven essays, respond specifically to MacArthur's *Strange Fire,* while the remaining twenty-eight, in the second section, are entitled "Classic Replies to Cessationism and the Misuse of the Charismata." The chief strength of the book is its excellent scholarship that will benefit a wide audience. Several of the chapters are scholarly, making ample use of New Testament Greek and exegeting in detail relevant passages; others, however, are written more popularly and can easily be grasped by those without formal theological training. Every chapter makes clear that the authors are not attacking MacArthur personally but instead answering his objections.

This review's brevity directs it to deal now with only several of the most significant essays. Asbury Seminary's Craig Keneer's review of *Strange Fire,* originally published by *Pneuma Online,* deals skillfully with MacArthur's theological arguments. Keneer acknowledges that some who self-identify with the PCM act in troubling ways and believe highly questionable theology, but he rightly rejects MacArthur's sweeping condemnation of the PCM as a whole for errors at its fringes.

Only one chapter of this work is written by someone who MacArthur might negatively characterize as a "faith healer." Randy Clark, founder and director of Global Awakening, travels throughout the world, praying for the sick and manifesting the gift of the Word of Knowledge. Likewise, he teaches others how to engage in the same ministry. Thousands who have attended Clark's crusades testify to receiving miraculous physical healing. Clark's chapter ably defends the contemporary practice of divine healing by appealing to Scripture and church history and pointing to MacArthur's "incomplete commitment to *sola Scriptura*" (59), because MacArthur argues almost exclusively against the practices and theology of the fringes rather than from scriptural exegesis.

The chapters of the second section expose the weaknesses of cessationism effectively, although several of the chapters include redundant content that could have been edited. Nonetheless, several chapters are veritable goldmines of important exegetical, patristic, and historical information. Robert Graves' two chapters adroitly answer accusations repeated commonly that those who claim to have been baptized in the Holy Spirit fixate on speaking in tongues or are interested in the ministry of the Holy Spirit more than in Christ's ministry. Graves's chapter on glossolalia is, in my opinion, one of the best treatments of the subject.

Strangers to Fire answers the questions that MacArthur and his theological allies raise concerning the PCM and its claims. Brought together in this one volume are finely crafted historical, exegetical, and theological arguments for the continuing manifestation of the *charismata* in the church, for the glory of God and the progress of the gospel.

Timothy B. Cremeens (PhD, Regent University) is Dean of Holy Resurrection Cathedral (Orthodox Church in America) and Adjunct Professor of Theology at King's College, both in Wilkes-Barre, PA, USA.

George Jeffreys: Pentecostal Apostle and Revivalist. By William K. Kay. Cleveland, TN: CPT Press, 2017. 461 pp.

*D*uring the 1980's, Pentecostal scholars Russell Spittler and Cecil M. Robeck Jr. challenged Pentecostal scholars to contribute to the corpus of Pentecostal histories by producing biographies of important Pentecostal leaders. Since then, many stories of early Pentecostal leaders have been produced and have given us glimpses into the history of the movement through the lens of its leaders' biographies. In *George Jeffreys: Pentecostal Apostle and Revivalist,* Pentecostal historian and educator William K. Kay tells the story of a prominent British Pentecostal pioneer, evangelist, and pastor. Weaving Jeffreys' story into his social and political context, Kay also gives us a skillful account of Pentecostal history in Great Britain.

Born in Wales, Jeffreys was the son of a coal-miner father and a mother who was the daughter of a Baptist preacher. After losing his father at age seven, George and his older brother Stephen became close as Stephen took over the role of head of the house. Between 1904 and 1905, the Jeffreys brothers were influenced by the Welsh Revival, during which George was healed of a childhood paralysis. George and Stephen both desired to enter the ministry and started preaching and evangelizing on nights in weekends. They soon gained fame as compelling preachers and began to hold meetings in Wales and Ireland and eventually all over England and Scotland. Kay documents the Jeffreys' effective evangelistic strategy, in which they held large crusades in rented venues and saw hundreds saved and healed. Following such crusades, Jeffreys would establish congregations with seasoned pastors and fund the purchase of facilities. This approach led to the founding of the Elim Assemblies, Elim Evangelistic Bands, and Elim Missions. In 1918, these various ministries operating throughout Britain merged into one of Britain's strongest Pentecostal denominations, The Elim Pentecostal Alliance. After several years of successful ministry together, George and Stephen eventually parted ways, and George rose to prominence through his strategy of using large evangelistic campaigns in London during the mid-1920s.

Kay draws interesting parallels between the events of Jeffreys' life and the rise and gradual decline of British supremacy between the two World Wars. At the height of Britain's colonial dominance, Jeffreys' ministry also saw its golden age, demonstrated by the successful yearly evangelistic campaigns held in Royal Albert Hall in London, 1926–1939. In an age of the great public oratory of Churchill and Lloyd George, Jeffreys' powerful preaching before large crowds won him fame as a British preaching icon. Several chapters in the middle of the book outline Jeffreys' books and his evangelical and Pentecostal theology expressed in the four-fold gospel of Jesus as savior, healer, Spirit-baptizer, and coming king.

In the final half of the book, Kay guides the readers through the challenges that arose during the 1930s. Through a series of disputes between Jeffreys and the Elim executive leadership, the organization Jeffreys had built began to unravel. At the center of the controversy was Jeffreys' push to adopt British Israelism, the eschatological teaching that God has a special end-time plan for Britain because the British are the descendants of the ten lost tribes of Israel. This decade-long struggle eventually alienated Jeffreys from Elim. Throughout this section, Kay carefully untangles the issues surrounding Jeffreys' eventual exit from Elim and his founding of a new organization, The Bible Pattern Church.

Kay's work expands on the limited biographies of Jeffreys from the past and expresses new research into the history of Elim and Jeffreys. At times the account borders on being too detailed, a possibility Kay addresses in his introduction. Even so, Kay's clear writing and attention to the pertinent historical context of the story makes the book enjoyable to read.

This biography of George Jefferies will appeal to those interested in Pentecostalism on several levels. It immerses students of Pentecostal history into the events and personalities of the first four decades of the Pentecostal movement in Britain. As Kay shows, what Jeffries accomplished as a mass evangelist, popular preacher, church planter, denominational and Bible School founder, periodical editor, and writer is on par with, if not exceeding, the accomplishments of some of Britain's most famous revivalists. This work also serves as a compelling denominational history of the Elim Pentecostal Alliance woven together with the stories of other Pentecostal denominations in Britain and Europe. For those interested in Pentecostal eschatology, Kay's treatment of British Israelism and the controversy surrounding its propagation demonstrates how eschatological ideas can shape the social and ecclesiological focus of Pentecostal groups. Finally, those particularly interested in British history will appreciate Kay's setting the story of Jeffreys and Elim skillfully in the context of Britain from the early 1900s through the 1940s. Pentecostals and all interested in twentieth-century British Christianity should treasure Kay's work on George Jeffreys for years to come.

Daniel Isgrigg holds the M.A. in Historical-Theological Studies from Oral Roberts University and is completing a PhD at Bangor University, Wales, UK, writing on the history of eschatology in the Assemblies of God.

The Revelation Worldview: Apocalyptic Thinking in a Postmodern World. By Jon K. Newton. Eugene, OR: Wipf & Stock, 2015. 380 pp.

*T*he last decade has witnessed a virtual renaissance in the academic study of the Book of Revelation by Pentecostal and charismatic scholars. The year 2006 alone saw the publication of three academic monographs devoted to the Apocalypse, including the first full-length study of its pneumatology,[1] an extensive examination devoted to the conversion of the nations,[2] and an investigation of the issues of religious identity in the book.[3] In the next few years these publications were followed by several commentaries devoted to the book.[4] During this time an important monograph devoted to the theme of worship in the book also appeared,[5] along with a number of significant articles[6] and not a few PhD theses on the Apocalypse currently being undertaken. It is indeed a wonderful time to be studying the book of Revelation from within the Pentecostal tradition.

One of the most recent contributions comes from Australian scholar Jon K. Newton (PhD, Deakin University), the Dean of Postgraduate Studies and Head of Research at Harvest Bible College and co-pastor with his wife of the Oasis Church in Melbourne. Newton is no newcomer to the study of the Apocalypse, having published previously a monograph entitled *Revelation Reclaimed: The Use and Misuse of the Apocalypse*[7] and having contributed articles on Revelation to a variety of academic journals.[8] While the trend to this point has been primarily either to offer a commentary on the text or to trace a significant theme or emphasis through the book, Newton pushes in a different direction altogether. He boldly proposes to identify and use the worldview found within the Book of Revelation as a foundational narrative by which to engage the sometime treacherous terrain of a postmodern world. This tremendously ambitious project is carried out in seven chapters—a good number for any Apocalypse project —with introductory and concluding chapters forming an inclusio around his more substantive work.

In the "Introduction," Newton creates for his readers the context of and need for the project by briefly defining what he means by worldview and describing the clash of worldviews witnessed in the contemporary postmodern world. He goes on to propose that a Christian worldview that is responsive to postmodern questions and challenges can be constructed but it will be one that has a distinctive voice in this postmodern context and not simply one that takes fully on board a postmodern way of thinking. In order to construct such a Christian worldview, Newton turns to the Book of Revelation because it is the book in the Bible most open to a postmodern interpretation, it is regarded as summing up much of the biblical story, and its foreignness may offer a way forward as how to live with competing worldviews.

Chapter 1 analyzes most helpfully the shift from modernity to post-modernity and its impact on biblical studies and Revelation studies in particular. Chapter 2 seeks to place Revelation within the religious and social context of first-century Asia Minor. However, unlike scholars who examine such matters with an eye toward issues of origins or influence or both, Newton compares the worldview of the Apocalypse with other worldviews of the day, for which he offers a measured and reasonable assessment. Chapter 3 attends to the reality of the Spirit World by examining the world of Revelation and engaging the contemporary context on such matters. Chapter 4 investigates the knotty issue of the phenomenon of revelation: prophecy, truth claims, and the criteria by which to discern truth from false (prophetic) claims. This chapter, in particular, focuses on numerous topics of special interest to Pentecostal and charismatic readers.

Chapter 5 focuses on the significance of personhood and analyzes nicely of its importance in the Apocalypse. Chapter 6 examines the centrality of the biblical story in a discussion of the place of history and meta-narratives within a postmodern world. Here Newton does a lot of heavy lifting arguing for, among other things, the place of history in the Apocalypse, the phenomenon of Revelation as story, and its relationship to the "Big Story of Scripture." It is here that the author explores Revelation as a war story and as a love story, concluding that Revelation—in a sense—can be seen as a Christian meta-narrative which can form a foundation for a Christian worldview.

In the final chapter, Newton examines Revelation's attitude toward rival narratives, some of which can be engaged and even transformed (Judaism and certain narratives of the non-Jewish world), others of which must be rejected (imperial Rome and idolatry). He concludes (308):

> Thus John shows us a possible strategy for Christians today
> in their response to other worldviews and ideologies of our
> time. . . . Christians . . . should not be afraid of claims that
> involve seeing the Christian story as framing and explaining the
> narratives of different cultures and providing them with a hope
> of fulfillment of their highest aspirations in Christ, albeit with

alterations and adjustments. Only the most blasphemous (that is syncretistic or imperialistic) claims need to be rejected utterly. In making these responses, Christians are giving priority to the Big Story traced in the Bible.

In his "Conclusion," Newton goes on to define a Christian worldview as follows (313):

> … a truly Christian worldview will always need to affirm the reality of the spirit world (with dualistic features), the validity of revelation (however defined) as a form of real knowledge, the fundamental nature of personhood, and the priority of the biblical story of creation, redemption, and consummation as an overarching explanation of human history.

Although quite an ambitious project, Jon Newton's monograph is, in my estimation, very important and contributes successfully in various ways to the Pentecostal and charismatic interpretation of the Apocalypse. Its strengths are too numerous to list, but a few of them must be mentioned. First and foremost is his extraordinary knowledge of the Apocalypse that he brings to bear in this study. Time and again he exhibits a very deep understanding of the substance of Revelation that goes far beyond the proof-texting approach that often appears in volumes devoted to this book of the canon. From this knowledge he is able to engage a variety of issues that always seem true to the nature of the Apocalypse. Second, he is to be commended for his honest engagement with a variety of dialogue partners. Absent from his study are the construction of "straw men" or "straw women" with which to dispense easily. He always appears to feel the full weight of the arguments he engages, even when he rejects or critiques them as lacking. Third, Newton has clearly demonstrated how a biblical book can contribute, at a foundational level, to the construction of a Christian worldview that has integrity and is open to revision as its contours are discerned further in the Christian community. Fourth, his extensive engagement with the Book of Revelation models a way in which this book, notorious for its abuse in the world of interpreters, can be engaged theologically with much profit in foundational ways for the believing community.

While there are any number of places where individual interpreters may have reason to disagree with this or that conclusion or inference, Jon Newton has contributed to Revelation studies significantly with this work, putting us all in his debt. It is to be highly commended. It is indeed a wonderful time to be studying the book of Revelation from within the Pentecostal tradition.

John Christopher Thomas (PhD, University of Sheffield) is Clarence J. Abbott Professor of Biblical Studies at the Pentecostal Theological Seminary in Cleveland, TN, USA and Director of the Centre for Pentecostal and Charismatic Studies at Bangor University in Bangor, Wales, UK.

Notes

1 R.C. Waddell, *The Spirit of the Book of Revelation* (JPTSup 30: Blandford Forum, UK: Deo Publishing, 2006)

2 R. Herms, *An Apocalypse for the Church and the World: The Narrative Function of the Universal Language in the Book of Revelation* (BZNW 143; Berlin: Walter de Gruyter, 2006)

3 P.L. Mayo, *"Those Who Call Themselves Jews": The Church and Judaism in the Apocalypse of John* (PTMS; Eugene, OR: Pickwick Publications, 2006)

4 R. Skaggs and P. Benham, *Revelation* (PCS; Blandford Forum, UK: Deo Publishing, 2009); G.D. Fee, *Revelation* (NCCS; Eugene, OR: Cascade Books, 2011); J. C. Thomas, *The Apocalypse: A Literary and Theological Commentary* (Cleveland, TN: CPT Press, 2012); and J. C. Thomas and F. D. Macchia, *Revelation* (THNTC; Grand Rapids: Eerdmans, 2016).

5 M. L. Archer, *"I Was in the Spirit on the Lord's Day": A Pentecostal Engagement with Worship in the Apocalypse* (Cleveland, TN: CPT Press, 2014).

6 One of the earliest, predating this renaissance by about a decade, is M. W. Wilson, "Revelation 19.10 and Contemporary Interpretation," in M. W. Wilson (ed.), *Spirit and Renewal: Essays in Honor of J. Rodman Williams* (JPTSup 5; Sheffield: Sheffield Academic Press, 1994), 191–202.

7 J.K. Newton, *Revelation Reclaimed: The Use and Misuse of the Apocalypse* (Milton Keynes: Paternoster, 2009).

8 Cf. "Reading Revelation Romantically," *Journal of Pentecostal Theology* 18.2 (2009), 194–215; "Holding Prophets Accountable," *Journal of the European Pentecostal Theological Association* 30.1 (2010), 63–79; 'Time Language and the Purpose of the

Millenium," *Colloquium* 43.2 (2011), 147–68; "Story-Lines in the Book of Revelation," *Australian Biblical Review* 61 (2013), 61–78; "The Epistemology of the Book of Revelation," *Heythrop Journal* (June, 2013), 1–14; and "The Full Gospel and the Apocalypse," *Journal of Pentecostal Theology* 26.1 (2017), 86–109.

Early Pentecostals on Nonviolence and Social Justice: A Reader. Brian K. Pipkin and Jay Beaman, eds. Eugene, OR: Pickwick Publications, 2016. 194 pp.

*I*n 1917, the prominent Pentecostal publication *Weekly Evangel* (now known as the *Pentecostal Evangel)* published a statement entitled "The Pentecostal Movement and the Conscription Law" that claimed that

> From the very beginning, the [Pentecostal] movement has been characterized by Quaker principles. The laws of the Kingdom, laid down by our elder brother, Jesus Christ, in His Sermon on the Mount, have been unqualifiedly adopted, consequently the movement has found itself opposed to the spilling of the blood of any man, or of offering resistance to any aggression. (93)

This position may surprise many in the current American political climate, when exit poll data from the recent presidential election suggest that the winning candidate—whose expressed views have very little in common with "Quaker principles"—garnered the vast majority of the white evangelical vote and has received very public support from leading Pentecostals. Indeed, "Pentecostal" is a word that has not been conjoined in the popular imaginary with either "pacifism" or "social justice" for quite some time. *Early Pentecostals on Nonviolence and Social Justice* seeks to change that by compiling 39 excerpts from 17 leading early Pentecostal figures, spanning the years 1901–1940.

Each author, in his or her own way, makes a biblical and Spirit-oriented case against the prevailing militarism of the period preceding the "Great War" and leading into what would become WWII. The authors include Charles Fox Parham, the influential leader of early North American

Pentecostalism, Frank Bartleman, the evangelist and journalist known for his chronicling of the Azusa Street events, Aimee Semple McPherson, social activist and founder of Foursquare Church, and William J. Seymour, the famed pastor of the Azusa Street Mission in Los Angeles.

The excerpts vary widely in quality and in intent, with some representing thoughtful extended reflections on the relationship between Christianity and the state (e.g., Arthur Sydney Booth-Clibborn), others offering practical advice on how to approach conscientious objection (e.g., Donald Gee), and still others making prophetic statements about the signs of the times (e.g., Parham, Bartleman). The best of the offerings come by way of the Booth-Clibborn family (Arthur Sydney and his two sons, Samuel and William), Ambrose Jessup Tomlinson, Aimee Semple McPherson, and the lay preacher from Kentucky, Elbert Carlton Backus, whose approximately three-page contribution is worth the entire price of admission. I'll share just one especially timely statement from Backus, reflecting on Christ's statement about giving one's life for one's friends:

> . . . let us pause just here to reflect that no love can possibly be Christian which is not universal in its scope. Christ loved ALL mankind, Christ died for ALL mankind, and although, in life, he . . . waged a fierce warfare, when he at last was ushered roughly into the presence of the Father, not one drop of blood stained his hands save what was all his own." (101–102)

The picture of Jesus one gets from these authors is unequivocally the infinitely loving, self-sacrificial lamb of God, slain for the sins of the world. The idea that this Man's teachings could be used to justify violence and oppression, even war, left these authors clearly bewildered. At one point, Gee remarks that "no Christian artist has ever represented the Galilean as commanding a machine-gun battalion or piloting a bombing plane. . . . [I]t has never been done simply because it is unthinkable." (136) Unfortunately, being "unthinkable" is a deterrent only for those who think; one can now easily find such "artistic" representations of the suffering Lord.

The few weak aspects of the book include the somewhat disproportionate focus on the work of Bartleman, whose views are occasionally interesting but more often problematic theologically or sociologically (or both), and the need for more careful proofreading in several places. But these are overcome by the rest of the work, which easily accomplishes its stated task, which is to provide a first-hand account of Pentecostal nonviolence and social justice. I cannot think of a weightier issue confronting the Church currently, and many of the authors' warnings are surely as relevant today as they were a century ago. In a review of another work from 1930 included in the volume, the *Pentecostal Evangel* stated, "Those of us who drift along unconcerned now that the sun shines, need to be jarred by this book." (143) We could say the same.

Robert K. Whitaker is a PhD candidate and lecturer in the Department of Philosophy at Marquette University, where he is completing his dissertation on the epistemology of disagreement.

Biblical Theology: Past, Present, and Future. By Carey Walsh and Mark W. Elliott, eds. Eugene, OR: Cascade Books, 2016. x + 233 pp.

A "selection of papers presented at the Biblical Theology section of the International Meeting of the Society of Biblical Literature over three years" (2012–2014; vii), with contributions from sixteen scholars, does not lend itself to a review of the entirety. The editors' organization of the chapters, however, provides an appreciated cohesion. Mark Elliott's "Introduction" is an *apologia* for the discipline of "biblical theology" (as distinct from systematic theology [dogmatics] or exegesis of isolated passages). "Biblical theology aims to see the big picture but to get there from an account of the details of exegesis of the biblical text. In that sense it can claim to hold the whole thing together" (x). Biblical theology, he continues, "will not abandon the spiritually important whole in order to stick with textual details or application, but will encourage the activity of shuttling between the two" (x). Not every biblical scholar cares for such "shuttling"; some question the relevance or possibility of "biblical theology." Whatever the reader's presuppositions, this book provides a history of questions raised and approaches taken, and an optimistic perspective on the necessity of "doing biblical theology."

Chapters 1—5 trace "historical developments" in biblical theology from the seventeenth through the nineteenth centuries (1–75). These papers perhaps hold greater interest for historical theology than for exegesis as such, but reflections from David Lincicum's essay on Ferdinand Christian Baur (nineteenth century) are important for exegetes and theologians (33–50). Baur's emphasis on diversity and conflict in early Christianity portrays "biblical theology" as "'a purely historical science . . . emancipated from the constraints of the dogmatic system of the church'" (35, citing Baur's *Vorlesungen über neutestamentliche Theologie*, 1). Baur's Hegelian philosophy may be passé, but his "critical method remains" (46), posing challenges to notions of a coherent "biblical theology" or an authoritative canon (36–43). Baur's critical method (still the mainstream of biblical scholarship) does not seek a unified "canonical" description of God and God's will for humanity.

The book's second section (chapters 6—11; 77–164) discusses "methodological considerations for biblical theology now." These enlightening papers are worthwhile reading for exegetes of either Testament. Several contributors interact with Brevard Childs and Walter Brueggemann, particularly their late-twentieth-century "biblical theologies." Those seeking to understand current variations in "biblical theology" may find Darian Lockett's paper (91–107) the most helpful in the collection. Lockett observes: "The problem is that there is little agreement on what biblical theology actually *is* let alone how to *do* it" (91). He describes (with their strengths and weaknesses) five distinct ways of doing biblical theology. His trenchant conclusion notes how they all illustrate "the abiding challenge for biblical theology, namely the relationship between history and theology in reading the Old and New Testaments as Christian Scripture" (103). Along the lines of Childs's canonical approach, Lockett argues that history and theology can both be respected by recognizing that canon "incorporates a historical process and theological judgment at the same time" (105). There is no choosing between history and theology; it must be "both and." Canonical "biblical theology" recognizes the legitimate interests of both history and theology—not neglecting one for the other but "maintaining the dialectical relationship between [historical] description and [theological] construction" (106).

Lockett's point is echoed in the following chapter (108–21) by Scott Hafemann: "The problem of biblical theology" is "the problem of history itself" (111). After citing Oscar Cullmann, Hafemann asserts: "To reject redemptive history as the heart of primitive Christianity is to reject the Christian message itself" (117). He concludes: "The point of biblical theology, therefore, is to reaffirm revelation in history within a robust view of the divinely inspired reliability of the biblical text itself, which will require restoring the humility of the theologian before the text and, supremely, before God, whose text it is" (119). Hafemann admits, "This will not be easy in a world bent on disavowing its own finitude" (119).

The theme of respecting the historically-situated text (and its theological ramifications) continues in N. T. Wright's chapter (147–64), which defends his approach to Jesus and Paul. "The Jewish context . . . is a non-negotiable element of the meaning of Jesus" (148). And "the so-called historical-critical school of exegesis" has "led us into a quagmire of false antitheses: *not because it was historical and critical but because it was not nearly historical or critical enough*" (151, emphasis in original). Sufficiently historical-critical exegetes should recognize the "non-negotiable" context of Jewish life and thought in the first century, particularly the theological themes of monotheism, election, and eschatology (156–64). Those familiar with Wright know the importance of those themes for him; those not familiar with him could read this chapter as a lively introduction.

The final section of the book looks for "constructive ways forward for biblical theology" (chapters 12—16; 165–233). Again there is variety. Janghoon Park (177–89) critiques Scott Hahn's "three-stage developmental view of God's trans-historical covenant-making" and Hahn's attempts to show how liturgical use enables Scripture's full efficacy. John Goldingay (203–13) suggests new ways of understanding narrative structures in both Testaments. Carey Walsh (167–76) contributes the volume's boldest essay, offering an astonishing interpretation of the divine speeches in Job 38—41. For Walsh, God's "whirlwind speech acts as a kind of conceptual idol" (170). This God is "almost a bully," lacking "signal divine characteristics" such as "love . . . [and] mercy" (173–74). "The wisdom of Job, then, is radically deconstructive" (172)—an understatement if Walsh's interpretation of Job stands. But since this chapter is an exercise in "Postmodern Biblical Theology," readers might deconstruct it as Walsh deconstructs (conventional readings of) Job.

This collection of papers (written for scholars) covers significant centuries in biblical theology and offers a stimulating variety of insights. The book's value is enhanced by the bibliographies included with each chapter (except for Wright's).

Arden C. Autry is an adjunct professor of Bible at Oral Roberts University, after a full-time career that included teaching at ORU, working for a local church, and founding a Bible School in Ireland.

Global Renewal Christianity: Spirit-Empowered Movements: Past, Present, and Future, Volume 1: Asia and Oceania. By Amos Yong and Vinson Synan, eds. (Lake Mary, Florida: Charisma House, 2016), xxxix + 498 pp.

This volume is the first of four that emerged out of the four meetings of Pentecostal and charismatic (hereafter PC) scholars under the sponsorship of Empowered21, an interdenominational initiative aimed at benefitting the global Spirit-empowered movement. The purpose of this volume is to study the historical and theological developments of Pentecostalism throughout Asia and Oceania, with the objective of understanding the challenges and opportunities lying before the PC churches (xxxix). The introductory note by editor Amos Yong highlights the diversity and plurality of the two selected regions of the study and overviews the five parts and twenty-one essays he and co-editor Vinson Synan have gathered.

In Part I: South Asia, Finny Philip (chap. 1) surveys the origins of PC churches in North India, with reference to the tribal Bhil Pentecostals, and investigates how their experiences impinged on their Christological understandings (1 & 15). G. P. V. Somaratna (chap. 2) discusses why PC growth in Sri Lanka was slow, if not stagnant, prior to the independence in 1948, and why it has progressed since independence. Thomson K. Mathew (chap. 3) traces the history and global growth of the Indian PC movement with reference to Kerala. He elucidates the transnational contributions of Karalites in global PC growth, and sums up with three points recommendations for further progress (63).

In Part II: East Asia, Robert Menzies (chap. 4) illuminates the enthralling experiential practice of Chinese Christian spirituality and the PC nature and growth of indigenous house church movement under the slogans of "China for Christ" (77) and "China is Blessed" (80). Iap Sian-Chin (chap. 5) traces the major contribution of Bernt Berntsen, a Norwegian-American Pentecostal missionary with ties to Oneness and Sabbatarianism, toward the establishment and growth of the True Jesus Church, an influential Chinese independent Pentecostal denomination. Yalin Xin (chap. 6) investigates "the inner dynamics" of the "Word of Life" movement from the perspective of Howard Snyder's "five-dimensional model of Pentecost" (110–122). Iap Sian-Chin and Maurie Sween (chap. 7) study the relationship between PC Christians with Protestant churches in Taiwan. Sang Yun Lee (chap. 8) examines the historical development and theological understanding of Korean PC Christians regarding the kingdom of God in both its present and not-yet aspects on the basis of the doctrine of the threefold blessing in 3 John 4 – "salvation, divine healing, and prosperity" (144). David Hymes (chap. 9) traces the impressive historical developments of the PC movements in Japan and highlights some of their theological trajectories.

In Part III: Southeast Asia, Vince Le (chap. 10) describes the origin, development, and current situation of Vietnamese Pentecostals, and concentrates on the issues of leadership, cultural engagement, and theological studies (194–95). James Hosack and Alan R. Johnson (chap. 11) trace the beginnings of Pentecostalism in Thailand with the arrival of foreign PC missionaries since 1951 (198) and describe the influence of the T. L. Osborn evangelistic meetings on the Thai PC movement (200). Timothy Lim T. N. (chap. 12) studies a distinct but healthy PC renewal in Singapore and Malaysia that began in the 1930s and continues to "shine and open up new frontiers" (232). Ekaputra Tupamahu (chap. 13) presents a critical-theological reflection on the works of American missionaries in Indonesia by focusing on the birth and development of Pentecostal Bible schools led by them (233). Giovanni Maltese and Sarah Eßel (chap. 14) present creative and penetrative theological analysis of transformational development of PC churches in the Philippines through a critique of Joseph Suico's 2003 PhD thesis (260).

In Part IV: Oceania, Denise A. Austin (chap. 15) explores how Asian Pentecostalism has helped form Australian Pentecostal identity. Shane Clifton (chap. 16) explains the beginnings and developments of the Pentecostal movement in Australia by concentrating on the three key trends of transitions. Mark Hutchinson (chap. 17) deals with the institutional tensions of Australian Pentecostalism (316) and argues that initial dilemmas such as the belief in *parousia*, gifts, ecclesial authority, and organizing principles are now the cause of a larger dilemma (329). Brett Knowles (chap. 18) reflects on the "glacial" change of Pentecostalism in New Zealand: from marginalization in its first thirty years to expansion in the 1960s and 70s to moral activism of the 1970s and 80s, with a numerical decline in this century accompanied by a greater "leavening' of mainstream churches" (340).

In Part V: Roman Catholicism and Other Theological Themes, Jonathan Y. Tan (chap. 19) studies the Roman Catholic Charismatic renewal movement in Asia, focusing on the Philippines and India. Jacqueline Grey (chap. 20) explores the possible influence of Chinese Confucian culture on Pentecostal hermeneutics. Simon Chan (chap. 21) analyzes possible directions forward for "Pentecostalism at the Crossroads," as it chooses how to adapt to culture, to respond to theological critique, and both to retrieve resources from the past and to update them discerningly in new contexts.

The editors preface the whole of the four-volume series with their evaluation, which this review endorses: the chapters arise from presentations at conferences and consultations, with a few commissioned separately. Most contributors, but not all, participate in PC Christianity, and those who do not were invited to write because of their known ability to discuss PC "with sympathetic objectivity" (xvi). The chapters thus evince some unevenness from the diversity of contributors' confessional stances and their varied academic and ministerial status; and the chapters, collected under such circumstances, leave many gaps in covering the whole of Asia and Oceania. This volume achieves, nevertheless, an important first effort of its kind in this generation to account for Spirit-empowered Christianity in these regions. It delivers historical assessment, theological self-reflection, "and even loyal criticism" essential for all students of PC Christianity. Such readers will benefit from "an expanded awareness of the challenges and opportunities" before this movement in these areas (xxxix). Highly recommended for students, ministers, scholars, and libraries.

Henkholun Doungel is a DMin candidate at Oral Roberts University and lecturer in the Department of Old Testament at Trulock Theological Seminary, India.

www.ingramcontent.com/pod-product-compliance
Lightning Source LLC
Chambersburg PA
CBHW070042100426
42740CB00013B/2760